To Change the World

To Change the World

CHRISTOLOGY AND CULTURAL CRITICISM

Rosemary Radford Ruether

SCM PRESS LTD

334 01677 0

First published 1981
by SCM Press Ltd
26–30 Tottenham Road, London N1 4BZ

Reissued 1992

Typeset by John Smith, London
Printed and bound in Great Britain by
Mackays of Chatham PLC, Chatham, Kent

CONTENTS

These chapters were first given as the Kuyper Lectures
at the Free University in Amsterdam in September 1980.

INTRODUCTION

No topic in Christian theology has been as exhaustively studied as that of christology. As the pivot of Christian theology, it is not only central to every theological reconstruction, but it is also subject to the constant revisions of historical scholarship. Because the centre of Christian theology is not an idea, but a person, a historical person, Jesus of Nazareth, what we can know about who this person was and what he did is of vital importance. The interconnection of historical knowledge and theological reflection makes christology vulnerable to historical criticism. If Jesus could be shown to have been a different kind of person and done different kinds of things from what the tradition has generally believed, this would be a matter of crucial theological relevance. So it is not surprising that some Christian scholars have expended all the ingenuity of historical method to ascertain as much as is knowable about this figure, while yet other traditions of thought have sought to shield Jesus altogether from historical investigation in order to make him apprehensible only to the believer by faith.

After this topic has been canvassed from every angle by Protestant thought from the 1920-60s, it is now the turn of post-Vatican II Catholic theology to take up anew the relationship of the historical Jesus to christology. Hans Küng in his major work *On Being a Christian* (Doubleday and Collins 1976) and Edward Schillebeeckx in his monumental tome, *Jesus: An Experiment in Christology* (Crossroad and Collins 1979) represent current post-Bultmannian trends in exegesis. These works exhibit the new confidence that historical-critical method can reveal the real historical Jesus back behind the kerygma of the early church.

1

Yet each of these works reveals the inescapable hermeneutical circle between the modern author's own values and *Sitz in Leben* and his reconstruction of the original Jesus as subject of the Christ of faith. The essential parameters of Hans Küng's Jesus reflect Küng's own position. Over against the political establishment and dissidents of his time, Küng's Jesus is 'neither right nor left'. Far from being neutral or 'above politics', this position makes Jesus very much like Küng himself, politically a supporter of the 'centre'. Yet Küng's Jesus is a sharp critic of the Jewish religious establishment. The confrontation between Jesus and the Law is basic for Küng's understanding of Jesus. Jesus is even said to have been 'crucified by the Law'. Analogies between Jesus' teaching and that of liberal Pharisees are dismissed with the words 'one swallow does not make a Summer'. Thus Küng appears somewhat insensitive to the question of anti-Judaism in the New Testament. His theological view demands a false and legalistic Judaism as the foil over against the authentic faith in God taught by Jesus. Must we not see here a reflection of Küng's own position over against the Roman Curia? There may be some danger in mixing up one's polemical portrait of the Roman Curia with a portrait of the first-century Pharisees!

By contrast, Schillebeeckx's Jesus is more irenic. Commonalities between Jesus' teachings and those of contemporary Jewish teachers are readily acknowledged. Schillebeeckx does not have the same need to contrast Jesus with Judaism. Jesus confronts no one. Schillebeeckx's Jesus is apolitical. He brings no judgments against the religious and social establishments of his day. He does not set righteous against unrighteous. His message is one of gratuitous acceptance of all equally. Jesus' death is not primarily a drama of betrayal by political authorities or by religious hierarchy. Rather, its deepest meaning is the expression of the unfaith of Jesus' own disciples. The resurrection reverses this betrayal by the disciples, especially by Peter. It is the faith-drama of Peter's repentance of his own lack of faith. Again surely we have here a reflection of Schillebeeckx's own personality and faith stance. The drama of Jesus confronts *us*, the disciples, with our own littleness of faith and need for repentance, rather than confronting political powers with their injustice or religious authorities with their hypocrisy.

To this author's mind, this hermeneutical circle between our contemporary values, concerns and faith-stance and our reading of

2

the Bible is inevitable. Those who claim to give us the fully objective and finally scientific historical portrait of Jesus only illustrate once again the close similarity between their Jesus and their own conscious or unconscious self-portraits. This does not mean that historical method cannot provide real parameters and limits about what we can say and cannot say about Jesus, and these have grown more precise through the labours of many generations of scholars. But there still remains a considerable space in which judgments remain, at best, probable, and the sifting out of earlier and later strata conjectural. In those interstices the portrait of Jesus will be rewritten again and again.

These essays on christology assume at the outset this hermeneutical circle between contemporary questions and interpretation of faith in Jesus as the Christ. Clarified hermeneutics lies in being conscious of the questions one brings from one's own situation and the response that one reads from the scripture, either negatively or positively, about these concerns. The questions which are brought to the scriptures in these essays are those which the author believes to be most pressing and inescapable for our times. To avoid or finesse these questions by declarations of neutrality indeed helps to perpetuate the problems. These are the questions of political commitment in the light of poverty and oppression, the question of anti-Judaism and religious intolerance, the question of justice for the female half of the human race, and the question of human survival in the face of chronic environmental abuse.

For Christians today there cannot be a final neutrality on these issues. One's portrait of Jesus' ultimately expresses one's own normative statement about the Christian message to the world today. If there is no connection between these two, then there is indeed no need to continue to speak of Jesus as the Christ or the gospels as scripture.

To say that Jesus was apolitical, neither left nor right in relation to the crisis of political power and social justice of his times, is finally to say that the same *status quo* detachment is acceptable for Christians today. To make the gospels essentially anti-Judaic is to give new sanction to the heinous history of Christian negation of the religious integrity of the Jewish people and their right to continue to exist as a people of God in their own terms. To say, as Schillebeeckx does, that the witness of all four gospels to Mary Magdalene's primacy as

3

witness to the resurrection is 'unofficial' and without kerygmatic content is not only to violate his own foundational principle that nothing is preserved in the gospels that is not intended by the early church to have kerygmatic content, but it is also to attempt to neutralize the whole question of women's apostolic authority. On a more subtle but no less vital level, we can no longer ignore the question whether our patterns of salvation and eschatology divorce us from our bodies and the earth or bring us into new harmony with creation.

These essays wish to ask about the relevant word of Christian faith for these questions of human justice and survival. Is the testimony of scripture and tradition concerning the meaning of Christ a part of the solution or a part of the problem? If indeed christology is a part of the problem, if the paradigms of christology perpetuate political detachment, religious bigotry, sexism and negation of nature, then we have to ask serious questions about the saving content of christology. A christology which is a negative sign on these issues is, in fact, not the bearer of good news or redemption for us today. Instead, it becomes a sanction for these very evils. We take neither our own vital commitments nor christology seriously if we do not confront this possibility.

Does this mean that scripture is merely judged, approved or condemned according to our contemporary values and interests? Does it now have a critical word to say to these values and interests? The hermeneutical circle between scripture and contemporary concerns must be a two-way relationship. We must be questioned by but also be prepared to question scripture. The strange and, in many ways, alien world of first-century Christianity does not yield readily to contemporary questions. Its presuppositions are by no means always ours. By searching in depth places where the world-view of the New Testament puzzles or confronts our assumptions, we can open up, again and again, transforming insights that expand our vision; such as, for example, Jesus' resistance to the title of kingship. We need to hold our values in some suspension, remaining open to correction.

Yet we cannot abstain from coming, at times, to a provisional judgment that the world of the Hebrew Bible or New Testament falls short of values which we must affirm. There are indeed tribalistic triumphalism, sectarian rancour, justifications of slavery and sexism in parts of scripture. The text then becomes a document of human collective moral failure, rather than a prescriptive norm. These judgments are not foreign to scripture itself, because, at these points, one can also judge scripture by scripture. The ancient texts do not preserve a uniform witness, but rather disclose a constant struggle between prophetic, liberating insight in changing contexts, and the sinful human tendency to devolve into accustomed patterns of status and to ascribe these to the divine will. This is a struggle that goes on within the biblical world itself, by which the prophets and Jesus criticize the religious 'hypocrisy' of their own community.

Thus our own critique of scripture for failing to live up to its own prophetic promise reflects and is rooted in the self-criticism that goes on in and is basic to biblical faith itself. It is on the basis of the same critical principle that we also search our own society and church traditions and seek to apply the prophetic word to our own world. The answer of Christian tradition to the vital issues of our times, then, turns out to be double-edged. On the one hand, we must confront the fact that scripture and theology have contributed to these very evils that trouble us. They have functioned as sanctions of evil. Yet we discover within the prophetic tradition and the gospels essential resources to unmask these very failures of religion.

We also find there revelatory paradigms by which to construct a redeeming vision of an alternative humanity and world. The teachings and liberating praxis of Jesus prove to be a focal point for this critical and transforming vision. Jesus discloses the transformatory and liberating patterns of relation to each other and, through them, to God, not only for his situation, but also in ways that continue to speak to our situation. For this reason he does not simply disappear into the past as a historical figure about whom we can know something, but who is ultimately unrelated to us. He continues to disclose to us, then, the Christ, the messianic humanity, whose fullness of meaning we began to glimpse in him and also in the signs of hope in our times, but whose ultimate arrival is still as much ahead of us in our day as it was ahead of him in his day.

I

Jesus and the Revolutionaries: Political Theology and Biblical Hermeneutics

New Testament hermeneutics, particularly in regard to the ministry and message of the historical Jesus, has become a new battleground, not just for scholarship, but for church politics.[1] Recent writings on the historical Jesus are characterized by much closer attention to the political climate of first-century Palestine. It has become increasingly evident that messianic prophecy in first-century Palestine operated as the expression of political opposition both to Roman imperial domination, and to the oppression of the Palestinian poor by the local ruling classes. The meaning of Jesus' messianic announcement, as well as the way it was understood by his contemporaries, must take much more specific account of this historical context.

In spite of all the rigorous attention to historical criticism over several hundreds of years, Christian writings on Jesus still have tended, to a large extent, to abstract him from his historical setting and to pay little attention to what certain ideas would have meant in the context of the Jewish world of his time. New interest in Jesus from the Jewish side may provide a new element here. The re-establishment of the Jewish state in Israel has caused a generation of Jewish scholars to identify with the nationalist resistance fighters against the Romans who died at Masada in AD74, and to see the state of Israel as picking up where these 'zealots' left off. Some Israeli scholars have begun to take a new look at Jesus as a Jewish figure in this critical historical period. The Israeli scholar Dr Pinchas Lapide has documented this new view of Jesus in Israeli textbooks in his book, *Is This Not Joseph's Son?*[2] Christian theologians, both

Catholic and Protestant, have responded to the liberation struggles of Third World peoples by taking a new look at the political content of the messianic tradition.

An exchange between three scholars of Christian origins indicates the continuing controversy over the political content of Jesus' messianic message. In 1951 the British comparative religion scholar, S.G.F. Brandon, produced a book entitled *The Fall of Jerusalem and the Christian Church*.[3] This was followed by two books, *Jesus and the Zealots*, in 1967[4] and *The Trial of Jesus*, in 1968.[5] In these writings Brandon looked at Jesus through the eyes of those political-religious resistance movements that led up to the Jewish Wars. Josephus' account of the Jewish Wars was seen as providing the context for understanding the messianic movements in first-century Judaism. Although Brandon did not go so far as to say that Jesus himself was an armed revolutionary, he did see certain figures among Jesus' desciples, such as Peter, the sons of Zebedee and Simon who, in Luke's Gospel, is called the Zealot, as having ties to the Zealot movement.[6]

Jesus is seen as a messianic prophet whose message carried much the same subversive and revolutionary message against Roman imperial domination as those other messianic prophets that dot the landscape of Josephus' account. These were the wandering messianic prophets to whom Josephus refers, in his hostile fashion, as:

> deceivers who claimed inspiration and sought to bring about revolutionary changes by inducing the crowds to act as if possessed and by leading them out into the wilderness on the claim that there God would show them the signs of approaching freedom. (*Jewish Wars* II, 264)

Josephus shows us that the Roman authorities regarded these messianic prophets as being just as dangerous and subversive as those who actually took up arms and led armed guerrilla bandits. For they fed the revolutionary unrest of the people by preaching the imminent advent of the kingdom of God. The Roman authorities regularly sent troops out to execute the prophets and cut down the mobs that followed them.

Brandon believes that not only Jesus and his disciples, but the early Christian church in Jerusalem, continued to be a part of this nationalist messianic ferment. This has been covered up and suppressed in the New Testament by the Diaspora and Gentile church which took over when the Jerusalem church was destroyed at the time of the Jewish Wars. This Diaspora church spiritualized Jesus' mission and deleted the political content of the messianic message in order to conceal the connection between Jesus' movement and the revolutionary ferment that led to the war of the Jews against Roman occupation.

Several scholars of early Christianity undertook to answer Brandon's views of Jesus. One of these was Martin Hengel, author of one of the major studies on the Zealots.[7] For Hengel, Jesus' message is the direct opposite of that of the Zealots. Every kind of violence, including revolutionary violence, is foreign to his thought. Jesus was pre-eminently a pacifist. Unlike the Zealots, instead of being a nationalist and religious purist, Jesus dines with the hated tax collectors and rejects the Jewish Torah in favour of a universal ethic. In his little book, *Was Jesus a Revolutionist?*, Hengel even says that Jesus does not take social or political oppression seriously.[8] The nearness of the kingdom of God has relativized all such questions such as Roman imperial occupation. What matters is inner freedom, the freedom of the nearness of God, which brings to an end the kingdoms of this world.

The New Testament scholar Oscar Cullmann also addressed Brandon's thesis in his book, *Jesus and the Revolutionaries*.[9] Cullmann admits that Jesus was crucified by the Romans on the political charge of being a messianic insurrectionist. This is the meaning of the inscription, 'King of the Jews', which Pilate attached to the cross of Jesus. Moreover, several of Jesus' disciples had Zealot leanings, not only Simon, but probably Peter and Judas Iscariot (whose nickname Cullmann thinks may have come from the word *sicarii*, or the sect of the Assassins, who executed collaborators with the Romans with short daggers, particularly in festival crowds). However, Cullmann would deny that Jesus himself condoned these views. He speaks of these disciples as 'former Zealots', on the presupposition that their joining with Jesus signalled their break with these kinds of political messianic hopes.

Cullmann, like Hengel, believes that Jesus was an 'eschatological radical' who believed in a transcendent kingdom of God that would be beyond time and history. This kingdom of God which, in Cullmann's view, Jesus thought was going to arrive very soon, relativ-

9

ized all questions of political institutions. Jesus accepted the legitimacy of the Roman state and enjoined the paying of taxes to it, for so long as it existed. But it had no ultimate legitimacy. It would soon be brought to an end, by God. But only God, not human efforts, could bring this world to an end and inaugurate the kingdom. Jesus rejected all political efforts to inaugurate a revolution on earth as a diabolical temptation. He preached only an individual conversion, and did not address changed social institutions. Such things belong to the transitory world that will soon come to an end. Yet his eschatological radicalism would be confused by his opponents, and particularly the Romans, with the Zealots' this-worldly messianism. This confusion led to his crucifixion on the charge of political messianism. In this sense his crucifixion by the Romans as a political messianic claimant was a mistake.

Cullmann believes that there were two different views of the Messiah at the time of Jesus. One was the official, nationalist and political view of the Messiah as a warrior and future national king who would preside over an earthly new age of peace and justice that would be inaugurated by God, but take place within history. A second view, found in the inter-testamental apocalypses and the book of Daniel, looked for a heavenly Son of Man to inaugurate a transcendent kingdom of God. Jesus subscribed to the second view, and identified himself with this transcendent Son of Man. One can get in touch with this transcendent kingdom through personal conversion. But one cannot prepare for it through any changes in the political and social order.

Cullmann comes out essentially in the same place as Hengel. Jesus' messianism is eschatological and personal. It has nothing to do with actual socio-political changes within history. Both authors, in fact, draw on the traditional Augustinian-Lutheran concept of the two kingdoms. Jesus' kingdom is spiritual, related to individual conversion. It does not change 'the world'. Although both authors wish to claim that this is a 'radical' and even 'revolutionary' position, such a view is fundamentally supportive of the *status quo*, since it effectively denies the possibility of any real change within history. The relativizing of all political options in the face of the kingdom of God basically means the levelling of all political options. Since the revolutionary option cannot bring us any closer to the kingdom than the present worldly kingdom of Caesar, the Christian raises the political and social questions only to negate them and return to co-existence with the present situation, but now with 'inner freedom', a 'changed heart' and presumably with personal charity for unfortunate people around him (or her).

One must ask whether such a spiritual and individualistic view of the kingdom can actually be regarded as a possible interpretation of messianic hope within the Judaism of Jesus' time. This is a serious question. If there was no possibility of such a viewpoint within any version of messianic hope that was available in the Jewish tradition, then one must ask whether the Christian claim that Jesus was the Messiah and fulfilled Jewish messianic hope is not and has not been an error. If a non-political and other-worldly view of messianism was not a Jewish option, then Jesus did not merely reinterpret messianism, he negated it altogether.

Brandon, as well as Cullmann and Hengel, seems to me to err by perpetuating the basic Greek dualism between the inward and the outward, the spiritual and the social, time and eternity. Brandon reduces messianism to secular politics and Hengel and Cullmann spiritualize it. But the dualism itself is inappropriate for understanding the messianic idea, which is *both* religious and political, both transcendent and this-worldly, both inward and outward. The kingdom of God is a holistic vision of this world, the created world as it is supposed to be when, as Jesus said, 'God's will is done on earth'. It means both reconciliation with God, when people obey God from the heart, *and* justice on earth and harmony between humanity and nature. These are not two different things, but, in fact, two sides of the same thing. There is no possibility of divorcing the two sides from each other. Reconciliation with God means the revolutionizing of human social, political relations, over-throwing unjust, oppressive relationships. The socio-political dimension is never lost in Hebrew messianism, but always remains the central expression of what it means to obey God.

The messianic idea is originally a religio-political concept. In most of the Old Testament the word Messiah, or God's anointed, does not refer to a future figure at all, but refers to the reigning Davidic king. This is the way that the term is used in the Psalms.[10] The king was seen as the mediator between God and Israel. As 'son of man' or paradigmatic human being, the king represented the community before God, and as son of God he summed up the election of Israel by God. The fortunes of Israel were seen as resting upon his justice and righteousness. His were the works, not only of justice, but also of mercy, the succour of the afflicted, the ransoming of captives.

As reigning kings failed to measure up to these expectations, the hope for a righteous king became focused on the future. Perhaps the next king would be the man after God's own heart who would do justice and walk humbly with his God. When the Davidic kingship was swept away by conquest and exile, these hopes could then be pinned on a vision of a restored Davidic king. At present Israel was suffering for her sins, but if she heeded the prophet and turned and repented, God would send a king to restore the fortunes of Israel. Like the ancient Davidic king at the enthronement festival, the restored Messiah would ride into Jerusalem on the white mule, both victorious and yet humble before God. The ancient promises would be fulfilled. He would command peace to the nations. His dominion would be from sea to sea and from the River to the ends of the earth (Psalm 72; Zechariah 9.10).[11]

As Israel experienced further adversity at the hands of the imperial powers, and also expanded knowledge of other cultures, the vision enlarged. It becomes cosmic in scope; not merely the restoration of Israel, but a new era of creation decisively different from the present. In some versions the nations, too, will share in this new age. Not all Jews were interested in a restored Judaean king. The Qumran covenanters centred their vision on a restored Zadokite high priest, to whom the Davidic Messiah is secondary.[12] The Samaritans had their own version of messianism focused on a restored Mosaic prophet.[13] A particular messianic figure was often ignored altogether. What was important was the messianic age. The messianic king was simply one possible symbol of this age.

In the book of Daniel and the apocalyptic writings of the intertestamental period, eschatological features come to be added. It is not enough for this new age to be enjoyed only by the righteous of the future. The righteous and unrighteous of the past must be resurrected so that justice will be done for all of human history, past as well as future. The interest here is primarily in solving the problem of injustice rather than the problem of mortality. Most of the apocalypses continue to assume that humanity is mortal. Even the resurrected are often assumed to be mortal. They do not live for ever, but only live that full life of long years that is the proper measure of redeemed humanity. We should not say that the apocalypses transmute the messianic vision into eschatology, i.e. life beyond death, but rather that they incorporate these eschatological elements into a basically historical vision and treat them as though they will be a part of a future historical era.

Possibly under the influence of Persian apocalyptic and Greek philosophical dualism, some of the later inter-testamental apocalypses become aware of the difficulty of introducing these eschatological elements into a this-worldly future era. There then develops what might be called the 'two-stage scenario'. For example, in one apocalypse we read that there will be a historical messianic age in which Israel's enemies will be conquered, her fortunes will be restored, and a messianic king will be born who will reign over a new era of peace and justice. Then the Messiah and all the righteous shall die, and the earth be returned to primeval silence for seven days. Then God will create a new and incorruptible world. Those who sleep in the dust will arise, and the judgment on the righteous and unrighteous will be revealed. This new age will have no end, but will be everlasting.[14]

The messianic and the eschatological often continue to be confused in apocalyptic writings. Sometimes one has a resurrection of the righteous in the messianic era and a second general resurrection in the eschatological era. But the trend of apocalyptic thought is to differentiate the two, to assign the Messiah to the historical era and life after death to the eschatological era. What is important for our discussion is this: once the two are distinguished, the Messiah is *never* associated with the eschatological redemption. The eschatological age is thought of as the direct reign of God. This is true of the New Testament book of Revelation, where Christ reigns over the millennium, not over the eternal New Jerusalem. Thus the basically political meaning of the Messiah is not only maintained, but reasserts itself in the apocalyptic development. From first to last the Messiah remains fundamentally a political figure, a future king of Israel.

Cullmann's assumption that there are two messianic hopes, a warrior-king Messiah and an eschatological Son of Man, cannot be sustained by a careful reading of apocalyptic literature. In those apocalypses where the title Son of Man is used, i.e. I Enoch, IV Ezra, this figure is also given the title and/or attributes of the

Messiah. Thus in I Enoch 46 the Son of Man is said to break the teeth of sinners, put kings down from their thrones, to be a light to the Gentiles, so that all on earth fall down and worship him; these are all clearly historical and not eschatological deeds. In the Son of Man vision in IV Ezra, the Man from the Sea flies on the Rock of Sion and emits from his mouth the sword of God's righteousness with which he slays the assembled armies of the Gentiles and gathers together his subjects into his kingdom.[15] There is no mention of resurrection or eschatological judgment. His deeds, however visionary, are basically those of a historical avenging warrior and future king.

'Son of Man', as a messianic title, has been much exaggerated in New Testament scholarship. The term means simply 'a human being'. As such, it can be used as a symbol of the Davidic king as the paradigmatic human being, or the collective Israel as the paradigmatic humanity, as is the case in Daniel 7. Or it can be used simply as a circumlocution for oneself, as when Daniel himself is addressed as son of man.[16] It was probably in this latter sense that Jesus refers to himself as son of man, contrasting himself with the foxes (i.e. the household of Herod) and the kites (i.e. the Romans). The foxes are thus said to have their 'holes' or palaces and kites their 'nests' or fortresses, but the prophet of Israel, Jesus, is a homeless wanderer in the present system of society. In these types of sayings, 'son of man' simply means I, the prophet of Israel. In those sayings where the term does seem to be used for a future messianic figure, it is clearly differentiated from Jesus: e.g. , 'whoever denies me will be denied by the Son of Man when he comes'. (Mark 8.38; Luke 9.26).

What kind of vision of the kingdom did Jesus have? In contrast to Cullmann, I would suggest that Jesus's vision of the kingdom was essentially this-worldly, social and political, and not eschatological. Jesus' views of the kingdom are expressed particularly in the parables. There is little trace in the more clearly historical sayings of Jesus of a predominant concern with eschatological features of resurrection, life after death and a transcendent world beyond history. On the contrary, his sayings suggest that his view of the kingdom remains primarily in the prophetic tradition, a vision of a this-worldly era of peace and justice.[17]

Of all Jesus' sayings, the one that most probably comes down to us close to its original form is the Lord's Prayer. Here the word 'heaven' is used as a symbol for the dwelling-place of God. But there is not the slightest notion that the kingdom means that we, human beings, are going to dwell in heaven. Rather, the kingdom means that the conditions of heaven will come down and reign here on earth. The kingdom, for whose coming Jesus taught us to pray, is defined quite simply as 'God's will done on earth'. God's will done on earth means the fulfilment of people's basic human physical and social needs: daily bread, remission of debts, which includes both the wrongs that we have done others, and also the financial indebtedness that holds the poor in bondage to the rich, avoidance of the temptations that lead us to oppress one another, even in God's name, and, finally, deliverance from evil. There is nothing to suggest that his vision includes conquest of death. The kingdom means conquest of human historical evil; the setting up of proper conditions of human life with God and one another here on earth within the limits of mortal existence.

Jesus' originality does not lie in his spiritualization of the kingdom, but rather in the fact that he saw the true fulfilment of its earthly hopes in a more radical way than many of his contemporaries. He did not see the struggle against injustice and oppression primarily as a holy war against the Romans. This does not mean that deliverance from oppression did not include deliverance from the Romans. But Jesus looked deeper than the oppression of Israel by Rome to the fundamental roots of oppression itself. He sees this as the love of prestige, power and wealth that causes people to seek domination and to lord it over each other. Unless this fundamental lust for domination is overcome, a successful war of liberation will only replace one domination with another. Jesus seeks to model, in his own life, a new concept of leadership based on service to others, even unto death. This is the model that he wishes to impart to his followers. In the new community based on the life of service to others, the lust for domination will be overcome at its source.

Jesus sees that many of those who ask the questions of liberation from Caesar are hypocrites, because they are themselves involved in the same international imperialism of money (to use the phrase of the Latin American bishops at Medellin) that they claim to oppose. This is the real meaning of his reply to the Pharisees on paying tribute money to Caesar. He sees that the Jewish élites are themselves a part of the same international economic system. They use its money and receive its benefits. His answer to them, while avoiding the trap of being labelled a Zealot, is basically a rebuke to the Jewish ruling classes. If you are part of the system of Caesar, then pay its dues! What belongs to God, for every Jew, was Israel itself, the land and the people. It is this that must be given back to God by establishing a new society of righteousness.

While Jesus does not primarily address himself to the struggle against the Romans, he also does not direct his message to the conversion of the Gentiles. In the manner of the Hebrew prophets, his is basically a mission to Israel. He can be opened up to the Gentile who surprises him with unexpected faith, but he does not hesitate to declare that his 'food' is intended for the children (of Israel) and not for the dogs; i.e. the Gentiles (Matt. 15.23-26; Mark 7.27). It is Israel, not Rome, that is the fulcrum of history. Through Israel's conversion, history will be transformed.

But this does not mean that his message to Israel is primarily spiritual, rather than social and political. The fundamental sins of lust for power, prestige and wealth express themselves fundamentally in social oppression. Jesus' critique of social oppression is directed primarily against the élites of his own community. These include the political élites, Herod and his family; the land-holding nobility, who reduce the peasants to indentured servants; and the religious élites, who use the temple and the Law to lord it over the unwashed, uneducated and outcast.

In direct rebuke to these ruling classes of Israel, Jesus denies his prophetic mission as a mission to the 'poor', both in the sense of those impoverished and crushed by debt in this system, and also those despised and reviled by this system of social status and prestige. He goes to all those who are regarded as having no hope of salvation within the present society, and preaches the good news to them. This good news is, socially, far more revolutionary than anything imagined by either the Essenes or the Zealots, much less the Pharisees or Sadducees. It overthrows the whole system of status through wealth, rank, education, and religious observance.

Jesus says that those who are outcasts, despised and without hope in this present world, will be first in the kingdom of God. God has been moved to particular compassion for them. Moreover, they will be able to respond to this message of God's prophet precisely because they have no stake in the existing order. By contrast, the righteous and privileged will not be able to hear and accept this message because they benefit from the present system. They will want their position in the future kingdom to be based on their achievements in the present social order. The Pharisee will expect to enter the kingdom of God according to his merits. The Essene will expect to take his place at the messianic banquet in accordance with the social and priestly rank that he holds in his community. None will consent to give up what they have, neither wealth nor rank, and enter the kingdom of God humbly behind the throng of the outcasts and unwashed.

Jesus' vision of the kingdom is one of radical social iconoclasm. He envisages a new era of God's justice and peace coming about only when all the systems of domination of money, rank and religious hierarchy are overthrown, when those who wish to be first are willing to be last and servant of all, and in which those who are nothing in this present system are lifted up. This is not simply a reversal of domination, but the overcoming of the whole structure that sets people in oppressive relationships to one another. Jesus addresses this message particularly to the poor, not in order to exclude the rich, but in order to make clear to them the conditions under which they will enter the kingdom.

The poor hear it and respond, but to get the rich to respond is like putting a camel through the eye of a needle. This does not mean that it will take a miracle to get the rich into the kingdom with their riches, but it will take a miracle to get the rich to give up their riches and accept the same status as the present outcasts and victims.[18] This is why Jesus is pessimistic about the response from the existing ruling classes. Not that he gives up on them. All things are possible with God. Indeed the risk of death that he took in coming to Jerusalem to preach his message was precisely his last effort to get these élites to hear his message.

The Romans were responsible for the crucifixion of Jesus, since it was they who authorized his arrest and carried through his trial as a political insurrectionist. Only they had the authority to execute him in this fashion.[19] The gospels, however, see the Jewish élites as morally responsible. This is understandable in the sense that it was to them that Jesus addressed his message and they who refused to heed him. Yet neither the Roman nor the Jewish authorities really 'knew' him. They acted from the perspective of their political

17

expediencies. In this sense, the only people who really could betray Jesus were his own disciples, for only they really heard and acknowledged his authority. The gospels tell us that indeed the disciples did betray him, not only Judas who sold him, and Peter who denied him, but all the disciples whose hearts continued to be fixed on dreams of power over their enemies. It was these dreams of power that caused the disciples to press the messianic temptations upon Jesus in his last days in Jerusalem, which resulted in his arrest and their own disappointment when these dreams failed to be realized.

The gospels are written from the perspective of converted betrayers, disciples who knew that they had been unable to hear the radical character of his message of abnegation of power in his own lifetime, and only in the light of the resurrection were able to re-evaluate this mistake. Yet we have to ask whether that mistake has not, in fact, been perpetuated by the successors of the apostles in the church. Even as the church picks up the cross as a symbol of triumph over death and as rebuke to the Jews, they continue the betrayal of Jesus, which is to use his name as a means of power and domination over other people. The Jesus who made himself one of the poor, one of the outcasts, and, finally, one of the dead, in order to witness to the true conditions for entering God's reign, witnesses against this betrayal of his name. He flees from those who use his memory as a means of power and domination. To adapt the Jewish legend, he is perhaps to be found among the beggars at the gates of Rome.

II

Christology and Latin American Liberation Theology

The recovery of the socio-political meaning of the messianic idea is central to Latin American liberation theology. Liberation theology wishes to reintegrate spirituality and material life. It seeks to overcome dualisms which have been traditional in Christian thought, but which are, in fact, foreign to biblical spirituality: the dualisms between faith and life, prayer and action, and daily work, contemplation and struggle, creation and salvation.[1] For liberation theologians sin means not only alienation from God and personal brokenness of life, but also the structural evils of war, racism, sexism and economic exploitation which allow some people to dehumanize others. Likewise salvation means not only reconciliation with God and personal amendment of life, but a commitment to a struggle for a transformed social order where all these evils will be overcome.

This commitment to a holistic vision in which the personal is integrated into the political has important implications for christology. Many of the earlier writings of liberation theologians did not deal directly with christology. This was recognized to be a dangerous area for conflict with the magisterial church. It was easier to speak more on a pastoral level than to spell out the revolutionary implications for the interpretation of Christ in history. Several major works on Latin American liberation christology have now become well known. There is the work by the Brazilian theologian, Leonardo Boff, *Jesus Christ Liberator,*[2] the El Salvadorean Jesuit, Jon Sobrino, *Christology at the Crossroads,*[3] and the Mexican theologian, José Miranda, *Being and the Messiah.*[4]

These writings evidence a different starting point for christology.

19

In Sobrino's *Christology at the Crossroads* various traditional starting points are reviewed. Liberation theology does not start first with a dogma about God becoming 'man' or divine epiphany. Nor does it start from the communal experiences of the resurrected Lord or of worship, or of the kerygma of Jesus, as in Bultmannian existentialism, or the teachings of Jesus, as in liberal moralism. Rather, liberation theology focuses first on the historical Jesus, specifically on his 'liberating praxis'. It is these deeds of Jesus that reveal the meaning of his person and his message.

Fundamental to Jesus' liberating action is his preferential option for the poor. Here liberation theology sees itself directly grounded in the mission of Jesus. The following of Christ must start with this critical option for the poor. The preferential option for the poor is not a matter of charity of the rich for the poor. It is not, first of all, the church who 'goes unto the poor'. Indeed if the ruling classes, and the church, which has been a part of the ruling classes, had opted for the poor, there would be no poor. They have chosen to oppress and exploit the poor in order to create a world secure for their own profits and privileges.

It is not we, the privileged (Jews or) Christians, but God who chooses the poor. God, through his prophet Jesus, acts in history by preaching good news to the poor, the liberation of the captives, the setting at liberty of those who are oppressed (Isa. 61.1f.; Luke 4.18). In so doing Jesus also reveals God's critical judgment against the rich and the powerful, the religious and social élites. The liberation of the poor becomes the critical locus of God's action in history. The movements of the poor can be seen as signs of the kingdom, as the places where God is acting in history. John the Baptist's question about Jesus' messianic identity is answered by pointing to this liberating praxis on behalf of the poor: 'The blind see, the lame walk, lepers are cleansed, the deaf hear, the dead are raised and the poor have the gospel preached to them' (Matt. 11.4; Luke 7.22).

Since it is the rich who have deprived the poor of all hope, God opts for the poor in order to right the wrongs in history. The poor and the despised will have a priority in the kingdom. Having nothing in this world, they will be particularly receptive to the good news, while the rich man will go sadly away. The pious and the educated will take offence at the messianic prophet, for they have been used to gaining status and power over others through their education and religious observances. For this reason it is said that the prostitutes and tax collectors will go into the kingdom of God ahead of the religious élites, the Scribes and Pharisees (Matt. 21.31).

This has nothing to do with romanticization of the outcasts or the assumption that the poor are righteous simply because they are outcasts. The tax collector, Zacchaeus, who was both despised and an exploiter in the imperial system, responded to Jesus by declaring that he would give half his goods to the poor and restore four-fold to those he had defrauded. It is for this response that Jesus declares that 'salvation has come to this house' and 'he also is a son of Abraham, for the Son of man comes to seek and save those who are lost'.[5] Thus those who are rich, even the exploiters, have hope if they hear the good news as a call to give up their false wealth and join Jesus in solidarity with the poor.

But the respectably privileged refuse to hear this message. This is why it is so hard for them to enter the kingdom. The message for them is, 'those who would be first must become last and servant of all'. Jesus exemplifies in his own life what it means to become a servant of all and to give one's life as ransom for many. Following Christ basically means to follow this kind of way of life in the concrete contexts of the social conflicts of one's time.

Liberation theology restores the kingdom of God to the centre of the Christian message. Like Jesus, the message of the church is to announce the kingdom. Christology and the church must be understood in relation to the kingdom. The kingdom means the overcoming of every evil, the wiping away of every tear. One cannot divorce social and physical evils, such as poverty, nakedness, homelessness, lameness, blindness, and diseases, from spiritual evils such as rejection of God, as though the social and material level was inferior and unimportant. Jesus manifests his liberating work in the realm of people's physical afflictions first of all. It is precisely in this physical and social realm that people's spiritual bondage and liberation is being manifested. To see that the world is full of outcast and afflicted people is to see that the world is at present in bondage to the Prince of Darkness. To see these afflictions being overcome is to know that the redeeming finger of God has come upon us. It is in this sense that the kingdom is already 'in our midst'. It is not 'within us' in the sense of an inward spiritual kingdom as distinct from an outward and social one (Luke 17.21).[6]

21

For liberation theology the kingdom is neither something that evolves from the present social system, nor is it unrelated to real social changes in history. It comes about through liberation, through the freeing of people from bondage to sin and evil and so is experienced as an inbreaking of grace. It cannot be incarnated completely in any particular social system. It transcends the limits of social systems, even revolutionary ones, and judges their inadequacy, pointing to the further hopes that are still unrealized. Yet this does not reduce all social systems and situations to the same level. There are some situations which are 'closer' to the kingdom than others, not in an evolutionary progressive way, but in the sense of signs and mediations of the kingdom which better disclose what God's intention is for humanity.

In our present world, when we see a society where a few rich families own almost all the land, where they suppress all protest with guns and tanks, where they manipulate religion and education to justify this exploitation, there we are far from the kingdom. But when we see the vast majority rising up against these evils, overthrowing the police state, beginning to create a new society where the hungry are fed, and the poor are able to participate in the decisions that govern their lives, there the kingdom has come 'close'.[7] It is in this sense that liberation theologians would say that some social situations and even some social *systems* are closer to the kingdom than others.[8] Some situations disclose greater justice and mutuality; some systems allow for greater justice and mutuality.

This does not mean that closeness to the kingdom is an assured possession of any particular system. A liberating situation can degenerate into an oppressive one. Those who made good changes on behalf of the people can gradually come to use their power to gain more and more privileges for themselves, and the last state of that house can become worse than the first. Merely claiming democratic or socialist ideology does not assure that you will do the things you claim to do, any more than claiming to be Christian means that one becomes a real follower of Christ. Closeness to the kingdom is a matter of concrete reality, not ideology or institutional privilege. It is a matter of discerning the realities of bondage and the realities of liberation that are actually taking place. This is why those who discern signs of the kingdom are prophets and not merely sociologists.

Nevertheless it is possible, in the midst of the limits and transitoriness of human existence, to make societies which are more liberating and less oppressive, and hence closer to the kingdom. To deny this is to deny all efficacy to God in history, to make the world solely the kingdom of Satan. The opposite of God's kingdom is not 'man's' kingdom, but Satan's kingdom. Both God's kingdom and Satan's kingdom are human kingdoms, societies of this world. The task of the follower of Christ is to move human society a little farther from the kingdom of Satan, the kingdom of alienation and oppression, and closer to God's kingdom, a society of peace, justice and mutuality.

By restoring the kingdom to the centre of the gospel, liberation theology also throws into question much of the language of finality that the Christian church has been wont to use about Jesus. We cannot speak of Jesus as having 'fulfilled' the hopes of Israel, for these were hopes for the kingdom of God. The kingdom of God has not been established on earth in any final or unambiguous form, either in the time of Jesus or through the progress of the Christian churches or nations. We cannot speak of Jesus as having overcome all evil or delivered us from all sin, as though that were a final and definitive possession that has only to be appropriated in faith and applied to some inward and invisible reconciliation with God. All this type of language mystifies history and betrays Jesus again to the extent that it turns us away from the concrete realities of good and evil in human life and teaches us that we can be saved apart from these realities.

The kingdom was present in Jesus' time, in those concrete signs of liberation, in those acts of healing and love that manifested the breaking of Satan's power over human life. But it was also absent in Jesus' time. The élites refused to hear him. His own disciples misunderstood him and sold him out. The Romans crucified him. The powers and principalities showed in Jesus' death that they were still in power. Christian faith, as resurrection faith, arises through a refusal to take these facts of the victory of evil as the last word. In the face of the assassination of prophets, Christian faith reaffirms that life and liberation are possible and God will win in the end. Jesus, the crucified prophet, thus becomes the name in which we continue to reaffirm this faith, his own faith, that the kingdom is at hand. But we affirm this faith not simply by verbal affirmations, but by following his liberating praxis and putting ourselves, as much as possible, in the place where he put himself, as ones who make themselves last and servant of all.

But this means that Christians, the church, can become followers of Christ only by knowing that they are, first of all, descendants of the betrayers of Christ. As successors to the apostles, the church descends from those who sold Jesus for thirty pieces of silver and betrayed him three times in the courtyard of the High Priest. We are descendants of those who pressed Jesus to seize power, to use miracles to display his authority and thereby to establish a new realm of domination where we could sit on his left hand and on his right. 'Get thee behind me, Satan,' Jesus said to Peter, the prince of the apostles, and the prince of the tempters and betrayers. The church continued to betray Christ by using his name to establish a new kingdom of domination, to rear up new classes of princes and priests, and to justify the subjugation of women, slaves and the poor. The kingdom of Satan is thus doubly entrenched in history, since Satan now wears the robes of Vicar of Christ and uses the cross of Jesus as his sceptre.

Liberation theology becomes possible only through a profound repentance of the church. It is therefore significant that liberation theology arises particularly from the church of third-world peoples, from the churches which were planted in the lands of black and brown-skinned peoples by uniting the cross of Christ with the sword of the Conquistadores. It arises from peoples who know what it means to be colonized; colonized religiously, as recipients of an imposed religion of Counter-Reformation Europe used as a tool of pacification of the poor; colonized culturally as peoples whose language and culture were stolen and replaced by those of the Conquerors, and colonized politically, as peoples whose vast poverty and political subjugation by repressive regimes is a tool of an international system of profit.

Yet liberation theology arises in Latin America from people who know that they are heirs of their Spanish fathers and not merely their Indian mothers; from peoples whose Catholic Christianity and European languages are a heritage to be claimed and transformed, not merely repudiated.[9] It was through this colonial culture that they also heard the good news of Jesus and learned to discover the real meaning of his message at long last. Latin American liberation theology arises from a church which is, first of all, a repentant church, a church that knows that it came as a part of a system of exploitation and acted for much of its history as a tool of domination of the poor by the rich.

As Catholic Christians, such liberation theologians as Boff, Sobrino and Miranda do their theology in profound recognition of the ambiguity of the church from its beginnings. They cannot skip over any part of this history and claim innocence of it. They have to deal with a church that refuses to be open to repentance by claiming to be endowed by Christ with an inability to err. They have to look at the way this church sacralized the power of Rome by merging the kingdom of Caesar with that of Christ. They have to trace through the centuries the way in which the church has made Christ the apex of a class hierarchy of rich over poor, men over women, masters over slaves, clergy over laity, nobles over serfs and finally Europeans over Asians, Africans and Indians. All the evils of the world from which Christ came to liberate us have been taken into the church and sanctioned through the Lordship of Christ. The cross of Christ has even been made the lynching post for Jesus' own people, the Jews.

How, then, does one discover in this church the gospel as good news to the poor? Because this same church is also the church of Latin America, the church of people who are poor, exploited and despised, who are the victims of these systems of colonization and dependency. It is by identifying with these people, their own people, the Latin American masses, that the church learns to hear the words of Christ and to become a repentant church. This means that this church has to speak not simply of personal sin, but of social sin, of sin as collective and institutionalized violence and greed. Social sin is of a different order from the sum of all the sins of individual sinners. It becomes a world which we inherit and which biases our opportunities, either as oppressed people or as privileged people, even before we have been able to make personal choices. This means that even people of good will do evil and profit by evil because of their privileged location in this system. This sense of social sin gives liberation theology a new understanding of the Christian doctrine of inherited sin, not as sin inherited through biology, but as sin inherited through society.

Liberation theology has to criticize many of the emphases in traditional theology, such as individualism, other-worldliness, the divorce of the spiritual from the social, the imaging of God and Christ as white, male ruling-class persons. These are not merely intellectual errors, but sins, the sins of idolatry and blasphemy. Tendencies of classical theology are recognized to be ideological (in the Marxist sense of ideas that justify social injustice).

There are two ways that the dominant theologies are ideological. One way is by directly identifying Christ and the church with the social hierarchies of this system and by making God the author and vindicator of it. The second way is indirect, more subtle, but has much the same effect. This is through divorcing religion from life, soul from body, Christian hope from human hope. In this way the message of liberation is alienated and directed to a never-never land beyond the stars which has no concrete implications for this world. Both of these ways of justifying the *status quo* are found in traditional theology, although the first tendency is found more in the theologies of Christendom, whereas liberal bourgeois Christianity tends to justify the *status quo* more through the second method. The gospel is thereby turned into bad news for the poor, Christ is made the founder of colonizing empires, and the church becomes an accomplice in oppression.

The repentant church is a church that has profoundly evaluated this evil history and knows that it can rectify it, not by words, but only by deeds, by concrete actions by which it puts its own life on the side of the poor and criticizes these oppressive ruling classes. The church which follows Christ must itself exemplify in its own life the preferential option for the poor. This means that it must be prepared to lose its privileged position in society, to become one of the persecuted, the tortured, the murdered. It must be ready to be a martyr church. For to follow Christ's preferential option for the poor in Latin America means to be ready to follow him into the grave.

The sign of the reign of evil in Latin America is not merely the reign of poverty, but the reign of death; the heaps of slaughtered peasants who are tumbled into a mass grave because they sought to organize a peasant's union; the bodies of tortured students, worker and peasant organizers found dumped in fields and rivers. The church in Latin America testifies to its determination to be the repentant church, the church of Christ, by following the poor not merely into their poverty, but also into their death.[10] Lay catechists,

26

priests, nuns, even some bishops join the ranks of the imprisoned, the tortured, the assassinated. It is from this reality that Latin American Christians speak to Christians of the First World, of Europe and the United States, about what it means to hear and preach the good news of God's preferential option for the poor.

This is why Latin American liberation theologians are often impatient with theologians from affluent societies when these theologians cavil at their views and accuse them of fomenting class conflict, teaching the identification of the kingdom with particular social systems or ideologies, or of being too immanentist.[11] These are judgments which liberation theologians regard as distorting their message fundamentally. They are not averse to refining their distinctions more carefully. But, for them, theology must be done, can only be done, by those who situate themselves in the reality of oppression, and whose theology is a reflection of liberating praxis. Those who do not do their theology from this context they suspect of not being able to understand what they are talking about. Their theological objections are screens against such involvement.

Gustavo Gutierrez constantly reminds Christians of the First World that the subject of liberation theology is not theology, but liberation. Christ calls us to be about the task of liberation, not about the task of theology, unless that theology is a servant of liberation.[12] There is no neutral theology, any more than there is a neutral sociology or psychology. Theology is either on the side of all by being on the side of the poor, or else it is on the side of the oppressors by using theology as a tool of alienation and oppression. This is why theology in Latin America is a serious matter, a life and death matter, and not simply an affair of the academy.

For Latin American Christians, it becomes evident that the real denial of God is not atheism, but idolatry. Many who think they deny the existence of God do so because they reject the abuses of religion. The ones who really deny God are those who use God's name to justify evil.[13]

The meaning of the cross, of redemptive suffering, also appears in a different light for those who suffer and are killed as part of the struggle for justice. Too often Christians have treated the sufferings of Christ as some kind of cosmic legal transaction with God to pay for the sins of humanity, as though anyone's sufferings and death could actually 'pay for' others' sins! Christ's cross is used to inculcate a sense of masochistic guilt, unworthiness and passivity in Christians. To accept and endure evil is regarded as redemptive. Liberation Christians say that God does not desire anyone's sufferings, least of all Jesus', any more than God desires or blesses poverty. Suffering, death and poverty are evils. God comes not to sanctify, but to deliver us from these evils. Solidarity with the poor and with those who suffer does not mean justifying these evils, but struggling to overcome them.

As one struggles against evil, one also risks suffering and becomes vulnerable to retaliation and violence by those who are intent on keeping the present system intact. This is not a question of violence or non-violence on the part of those who struggle. Non-violent struggle is no protection against unjust violence in a system which is maintained by unjust violence. But in risking suffering and even death on behalf of a new society, we also awaken hope. The poor learn not to be afraid of those in power and to begin to take their destiny into their own hands. Even when the prophet is killed, the struggle goes on. Indeed, their very death becomes a rallying point for new energy. In their name people now organize themselves to renew the work of liberation. The memory of their lives becomes stronger than the powers of death and gives people hope that the powers of death can be broken. This is the real meaning of redemptive suffering, of Jesus and of Christians, not passive or masochistic self-sacrifice.

The suffering and death of the just also raises the question of theodicy. Why does a just and all-powerful God permit the good to suffer? If God can deliver us from evil, why doesn't 'he' do so?[14] Christians begin to rediscover the stark meaning of the cry of Jesus from the cross: 'My God, my God, why hast thou forsaken me?' The messianic prophet has given his life as ransom for many, has preached good news to the poor, has healed the afflicted. But the powers and principalities are not changed. They close in on him and string him up from the gallows of their false justice. As his blood is poured out, he scans the sky looking for the hand of God. But the heavens remain closed. God does not reach down to draw his prophet out of many waters and deliver him from his enemies.

Does the resurrection allow us simply to deny this cry from the cross? Do we say that Jesus did not really intend this as a cry of despair, that all along he knew that God would raise him up on the

28

third day? Too often Christians use the resurrection as a way of not taking the unresolved evils of history seriously. We forget that the cross is not initially a symbol of the victory of God, but a victory for the powers and principalities. We transform it into a symbol of the victory of God only if we deny this victory of evil by continuing Jesus' struggle against it. We should not stifle the cry of Jesus by spiritualizing this victory over death, but, instead, let it continue to ring out from the cross, from all the crosses of unjust suffering throughout history, as a question mark about the nature of present reality.

Who, then, is really in charge of history: God or Satan? If we say that God is really the author of this unjust history, that God is merely using it to test us, or that he has abdicated for a while only to intervene later, we make a mockery of the death of martyrs. Perhaps this whole concept of God as omnipotent sovereign is thrown into question by the death of Christ, by the martyrdom of the just. Such a God is modelled after the powers of domination. When we model our God after emperors and despots who reduce others to dependency, then we have a problem of theodicy. But the cross of Jesus reveals a deeper mystery. The God revealed in Jesus has identified with the victims of history and has abandoned the thrones of the mighty. In Jesus' cross God abandons God's power into the human condition utterly and completely so that we might not abandon each other. God has become a part of the struggle of life against death. This is perhaps why those who struggle for justice do not ask the question of theodicy. They know that the true God does not support the thrones of the mighty, but is one of them.[15]

While the church which opts for the poor is primarily a critic of the unjust powers, it must also be a critic of the 'project of the poor'.[16] In Latin America this is not primarily a question of violence versus non-violence. Latin Americans are bemused by the obsession of First-World Christians with this issue. In Chile, Brazil, El Salvador and Nicaragua there exists a situation of total violence. So there is no way to protest or struggle without evoking violence. Violence is already the dominant reality. The Christian should be primarily with those who suffer rather than those who inflict suffering, even on the oppressors. But in real struggle, there is no way to keep one's hands clean.[17]

Rather, the real point of danger comes when victory becomes

possible. How can one avoid the temptation of the victorious poor to become the avengers? Is it possible to dethrone the mighty and still redeem them as brothers and sisters? How does one really root out a system of oppression and yet still exercise forgiveness and reconciliation towards those who have tortured and murdered the people? Here is where the Christian character of the struggle is really tested. The Christian begins to understand Jesus' own struggle against messianic temptation. Here the church learns to pray with Jesus, 'Lead us not into temptation, but deliver us from evil.'

There are two temptations to be avoided. One is simply to seize power in a way that absolutizes one's own victory and identifies it with truth against all critics. In this fashion revolutions quickly turn into new oppressions. The other temptation is to fear to become involved at all, to prefer failure and death rather than to risk real efficacy. God does not desire death, but new life and new possibilities for human community. The Christian, when the time comes, must also risk taking power and seek to use it for service rather than domination.

Yet there are perhaps different roles that are appropriate for church officials at this point. The Pope may be right, although for the wrong reasons. Maybe priests and nuns should not hold political office, but leave that for others. This is not because the official church should not be involved in politics, for we are never uninvolved in politics, but rather that the Christian who holds church office should use that office primarily to stay at the grass roots with the poorest in their day-to-day needs. In this way the church will avoid the temptation to idealize a particular situation, not to deny the possibility of real change, but to encourage it by keeping the revolution honest.

The struggle is always unfinished; there is still more that needs to be done. It is at this point of the unfinished business of good and evil that the church needs to find its primary point of incarnation. It does so, not to reject the revolution, but to keep it in creative and self-critical struggle. The church can do this with credibility only if it puts its own life into the struggle. As the lesson of Cuba has shown, a church which has not participated in the revolution cannot be the conscience of the revolution.

III

Christology and Jewish-Christian Relations

The antisemitic heritage of Christian civilization is neither an accidental nor a peripheral element. It cannot be dismissed as a legacy from 'paganism', or as a product of purely sociological conflicts between the church and the synagogue.[1] Antisemitism in Western civilization springs, at its root, from Christian theological anti-Judaism. It was Christian theology that developed the thesis of the reprobate status of the Jew in history and laid the foundations for the demonic view of the Jew which fanned the flames of popular hatred. This hatred was not only inculcated by Christian preaching and exegesis. It became incorporated into the structure of Canon Law and also the civil law formed under the Christian Roman emperors, such as the Codes of Theodosius (AD 420) and of Justinian (sixth century). These anti-Judaic laws of the church and the Christian empire laid the basis for the debasement of the civic and personal status of the Jew in Christian society that lasted until the emancipation in the nineteenth century. These laws were, in part, revived in the Nazi Nuremberg laws of 1933.[2]

The understanding of christology is, I believe, at the heart of the problem. Theologically, anti-Judaism developed as the left hand of christology. Anti-Judaism was the negative side of the Christian affirmation that Jesus was the Christ. Christianity claimed that the Jewish tradition of messianic hope was fulfilled in Jesus. But since the Jewish religious teachers rejected this claim, the church developed a polemic against the Jews and Judaism to explain how the church could claim to be the fulfilment of a Jewish religious tradition when the Jewish religious teachers themselves denied this.

At the root of this dispute lies a fundamentally different understanding of the messianic idea that developed in Christianity, in

31

contrast to the Hebrew scriptures and the Jewish teaching tradition. Judaism looked to the messianic coming as a public, world-historical event which unequivocally overthrew the forces of evil in the world and established the reign of God. Originally Christianity also understood Jesus' messianic role in terms of an imminent occurence of this coming reign of God. But when this event failed to materialize, Christianity pushed it off into an indefinite future, i.e. the Second Coming, and reinterpreted Jesus' messianic role in inward and personal ways that had little resemblance to what the Jewish tradition meant by the coming of the Messiah. An impasse developed between Christianity and Judaism, rooted in Christian claims to messianic fulfilment and supercession of Judaism, that were not only unacceptable but incomprehensible in the Jewish tradition. The real difference between these two views has never really been discussed between Christians and Jews in any genuine fashion because, at an early stage of development, these growing differences of understanding of the messianic advent were covered over with communal alienation and mutual polemic.

Christian teachers sought to vindicate their belief in Jesus as the Christ by reinterpreting Hebrew prophecy to accord with the Christian view of Christ. This Christian exegesis also denied the ability of the Jewish teachers to interpret their own scriptures. The Jews, Christians said, had always been apostate from God and their teachers spiritually blind and hard of heart. In effect, Christian theology set out to demonstrate the rejected status of the Jewish people and the spiritual blindness of its exegesis and piety in order to vindicate the correctness of its own exegesis and its claim to be the rightful heir of Israel's election.

According to Christian teaching, it is the church which is the true heir to the promises to Abraham. It is the spiritual and universal Israel, foretold by the prophets, while the Jews are the heirs of an evil history of perfidy, apostasy and murder. As a result, the Jewish people have been cut off from their divine election. Divine wrath has been poured down on them in the destruction of the temple and the national capital city of Jerusalem. They have been driven into exile and will be under a divine curse as wanderers and reprobates until the end of history, when Jesus returns as the Christ and the Jews finally have to acknowledge their error.

In effect, the church set up its polemic against the Jews as a historical task of Christians to maintain perpetually the despised status of the Jews as a proof of their divine reprobation. At the same time, the church taught that the Jews must be preserved to the end of history as 'witness' to the ultimate triumph of the church.[3] This theological stance was expressed in the official policy of the church towards the Jews through the centuries, combining social denigration with pressure for conversion. It also unleashed waves of hatred and violence that were seldom controllable within the official church policy of minimal protection of Jewish survival. In Nazism the Christian demonization of the Jews' spiritual condition was converted into a demonization of their biological condition. Hence the Nazi final solution to the Jewish question was not religious conversion, but physical extermination, to make way for the millennium of the Third Reich.

For us, who live after the Holocaust, after the collapse of Christian eschatology into Nazi genocidal destruction, profound reassessment of this whole heritage becomes necessary. Although Nazis hated Christians as well as Jews, the church nevertheless must take responsibility for the perpetuation of the demonic myth of the Jew that allowed the Nazis to make the scapegoat of their project of racial purity.[4] This Christian tradition also promoted an antipathy in Christians who too often felt little need to respond to the disappearance of their Jewish neighbours. We have to examine the roots of the theological patterns that fed this demonic myth of the Jew and its perpetuation, even in liberal theologies, today.

In this chapter I shall examine three basic theological patterns that promote anti-Judaism. I shall discuss how these dualistic patterns of Christian faith and negation of Judaism have operated historically. I shall also present critical reconstructions of these theses, I hope freed from their anti-Jewish bias. Then I shall focus on christology as the centre around which all these dualisms cluster, and ask how christology itself has to be reconstructed in the light of these criticisms.[5]

1. *The schism of judgment and promise*

The Christian *Adversus Judaeos* tradition was built on a two-sided exegesis of the Hebrew scriptures. On the one hand, Christian *midrash* of the Psalms and Prophets sought to show that the scriptures predicted Jesus as the Christ, and also that they demonstrated the perfidy of the Jews and predicted their final apostasy. This exegesis was developed by Christian teachers before the written New Testament as a part of the oral tradition of Christian catechetics. It was incorporated into the exegesis and theology of the New Testament. The argument continued as a proof-texting tradition into the patristic period. Writings against the Jews in the corpus of the church fathers continued to be built on a tradition of christological and anti-Judaic proof-texts. This exegetical tradition shows the close connection between christology and anti-Judaism.[6]

This type of exegesis distorted fundamentally the meaning of prophetic criticism. The dialectical structure of prophetic thought was split apart, so that its affirmative side, of forgiveness and promise, was assigned to the Christian church, while its negative side, of divine wrath and rejection, was read out against the Jews. This splitting of the left hand of prophetic criticism from the right hand of hope and promise creates an unrelieved caricature of evil projected upon another people with whom the Christian no longer identifies. The church thereby divorced herself from the heritage of prophetic self-criticism and stands triumphant and perfect. The Hebrew scriptures, which actually contain the tradition of Jewish religious self-criticism and repentance, is turned into a remorseless denunciation. All the evils condemned by the prophets are seen as characteristic of this perfidious people. Anti-Judaism and ecclesiastical triumphalism arise as two distortions of a false polarization of the prophetic dialectic.

This ancient Christian tradition of exegesis has practically disappeared among Old Testament scholars. Most Christian scholars of Hebrew scripture interpret them historically, and not as predictions of Jesus as Christ. This also leaves largely unexplained the theological claim that the New Testament 'fulfils' the Old (the term Old Testament itself, of course, reflects a christological and anti-Judaic interpretation of Hebrew scripture).

A more difficult problem occurs in the New Testament. Here anti-Judaic exegesis has been woven into the very patterns of theological interpretation and put into the mouth of Jesus himself. I will confine my remarks to the denunciations of the Scribes and Pharisees that occur in the synoptic gospels. I suggest that here we see two different stages of development. In the first stage, in the ministry of Jesus, there is a denunciation of hypocritical religion that stands in the authentic line of Hebrew prophecy. As the prophet Amos cried out against externalized ritual:

I hate, I despise your feasts, and I take no delight in your solemn assemblies ... Take away from me the noise of your songs; to the melody of your harps I will not listen. But let justice roll down the waters, and righteousness like an ever-flowing stream. (Amos 5.21, 23f.)

so the Jesus of the synoptics cries out:

Woe to you, Scribes and Pharisees, hypocrites! for you tithe mint and dill and cummin, and have neglected the weightier matters of the law, justice and mercy and faith; these you ought to have done, without neglecting the others. (Matt. 23.23)

Such denunciations are not rejections of Judaism, but are built upon Judaism itself. They presuppose Hebrew faith and existence within the covenant of Israel. The Matthew passage does not in any way reject the Torah. It stands within the debate of rabbinic schools of Jesus' time about the priorities for interpreting and following the Torah.

A second stage occurs when the Christian church comes to perceive itself as a fundamentally new covenant founded on the new way of salvation, Christ, that supersedes the Torah and renders it obsolete and inferior. Then the prophetic critique of hypocritical ways of living the Law come to be read as a denunciation of the Law itself as *essentially* hypocritical. The criticism of bad scribes and Pharisees is taken to be a rejection of all Jewish scribes and Pharisees as essentially teachers of this bad religion rejected by Jesus.

The shift from one to the other may appear subtle, but, in fact, it is fundamental. In contemporary terms it would be the difference between a person who denounces a patriarchal reading of christology and a person who denounces christology as essentially patriarchal and calls for all people who desire justice to leave the Christian church and found a new religion based on a different soteriological principle. The first person remains within the Christian tradition, however many Christians may find what is said unacceptable.

35

The second person has chosen to reject the Christian community as a context of identity.

The Jesus who announced a coming reign of God and preached to the poor in a manner critical of religious élites was undoubtedly a radical and controversial figure, but not one who stood in any way outside the Jewish tradition. Contemporary Jewish scholars have no difficulty affirming this Jesus as a part of the spectrum of Jewish controversy over the Law and the Kingdom in the first century. But the Christ of Christian faith, whose messianic hope has been translated into a supersessionary principle over against the Torah, is a figure that departs fundamentally from the ground of peoplehood in Israel. He has become the basis of an anti-Judaic gospel.

There is no way to retrace this historical path and assume literally the stance of Jesus as prophetic critic and messianic proclaimer in the Judaism of his day. If the 998 million Christians were suddenly to apply to re-enter Judaism, the 14 million surviving Jews would certainly not know what to do with us. Rather, we must reconstruct the stance of Jesus in a way appropriate to our own historical condition.

There are two elements in a correction of the anti-Jewish reading of Jesus' criticism of religion. On the one hand, we must recognize that prophetic criticism is always internal criticism, a criticism that springs from loyalty and commitment to the true foundations of the people whom you criticize. It is fundamentally distorted when it becomes simply the repudiation of another people who are no longer your own. Therefore whatever is valid in the denunciation of legalism and hypocrisy in the gospels must be appropriated by Christians as self-criticism. We must translate words such as 'scribes' and 'Pharisees' into words such as 'clerics' and 'theologians'. Since most of us who have the chance to do that are ourselves clerics and/or theologians, it should be evident that what is being criticized is not Christianity or even Christian leadership, but certain false ways of setting up leadership that crushes the message of the gospel. We might remember that Jesus himself was called 'Rabbi' by his apostles.

This kind of internalization of the gospel critique of religion is already quite common in Christian theology and preaching. Many liberal and liberation theologians, such as Hans Küng or Leonardo Boff, put particular emphasis on this denunciation of false religion precisely for the purpose of criticizing fossilized hierarchical religion within their own religious communities.

However, this internalization of the gospel criticism of religion will not overcome the anti-Judaic stereotype unless we are willing to concede to the Judaism of Jesus' day the same religious validity that we attribute to our own Christian faith. Surely we expect our own religion not only to survive, but to be purified through such criticisms? If Hans Küng does not think that he becomes anti-Catholic because he denounces hypocritical hierarchicalism in the Catholic Church, then he should not assume that Jesus fundamentally departs from the ground of Torah and Israel when he makes a similar denunciation of false teachers.[7]

This second principle is seldom observed by Christian scholars. Again and again we find Christian theologians, not just conservatives, but theologians on the Left, who are happy to use the gospel denunciations to criticize legalistic tendencies in their own community. Yet they continue to write as though these bad traits, which are only distortions of *their* faith, are somehow *generic* to Judaism. Indeed such anti-Judaism becomes reasserted and defended by liberal and liberation thinkers, as though the purging of the shadow side of their own faith still demanded the Jewish scapegoat as its point of reference.[8]

This negative projection of Christian self-criticism on to Judaism cannot be corrected without a positive appreciation of Judaism, of the rabbinic tradition and Jesus' place in the Judaism of his time. Christians must discover that leaders of the Pharisaic schools, such as Hillel, were making some of the same interpretations of the Law as did Jesus; i.e. that love of the neighbour is the essence of the Law.[9] Christians must correct the stereotype use of the word 'Pharisee'. Only then will Christian exegetes and preachers be prepared to translate the New Testament language into the same kind of nuanced appreciation of Jesus' Judaism that they would expect to convey about their own Christianity; namely, a religion that contains the possibilities both of prophetic vision and of institutional deformation.

2. *The schism of particularism and universalism*

Christians have seen their faith as the universal religion, superseding the particularism of Judaism. Paul's 'neither Jew nor Greek' is seen as the great breakthrough from tribal religion to the religion of universal humanity. Christianity fulfils the messianic promise of the ingathering of all nations, as opposed to the particularistic identification of Israel with one people and one land. It is true that particularism, even in the Hebrew scriptures, sometimes becomes simply ingrown ethnocentricity and animosity to others. But what has been less apparent to Christians is the way that universalism can become imperialism towards all other peoples. Christianity has seen itself as the *only* valid, redemptive identity. All other religious identities are seen as spurious, demonic and lacking true relationship to God. To be saved, all must incorporate themselves into the one true human identity, the Christian faith. Even modern liberal theologians, such as Bultmann or Küng, speak of Christianity as 'authentic humanity' without asking whether this means that all other peoples have an inauthentic humanity.[10] The missionary who viewed non-Christians as 'devil-worshippers' did not always avoid translating this theological judgment into a racial judgment on the inferior nature of non-Christian peoples. The mandate to conquer and subdue all nations often went hand in hand with the mandate to convert all nations.

Such imperialist universalism fails to be authentically universalist. It actually amounts to the absolutization of one particularism. In this respect Christianity can learn something from the very different way in which Judaism has understood universalism. Judaism has seen itself as having a universal mission to enlighten other nations about higher religion, expressed particularly in monotheism and the basic code of ethics, i.e., the Noachic code, as distinct from the Torah.[11] Although Judaism is open to the true proselyte, it has not seen its mission primarily as conversion of others to Judaism. This is both because Judaism sees its special characteristics as given to a particular people rather than to all people, and also because it believed that the 'righteous Gentile' could be saved in his or her own religion.[12] Conversion to Judaism is not necessary for salvation. These views lay the basis for a self-limited particularism that, potentially, recognizes the rights of other peoples to define their own identity and relation to God in terms of their own religious culture.

True universalism must be able to embrace existing human pluralism, rather than trying to fit every people into the mould of religion and culture generated from one historical experience. Only God is one and universal. Humanity is finally one because the one God created us all. But the historical mediators of the experience of God remain plural. There is no final perspective on salvation available through the identity of only one people, although each people's revelatory point of reference expresses this universal in different contexts. Just as each human language points more or less adequately to universal truths, and yet is itself the product of very particular peoples and their histories, so religions are equally both bearers of universal truth and yet particular in form. To impose one religion on everyone flattens and impoverishes the wealth of human interaction with God, much as imposing one language on everyone steals other peoples' cultures and memories. If there is a messianic 'end point' of history that gathers up all these heritages into one, it can only happen through incorporating them all, not through suppressing them all in favour of the experience of one historical group. In order to be truly catholic, Christians must revise the imperialistic way they have defined their universality.

3. *The schisms of law and grace; letter and spirit; old and new Adam*

Classical Christian theology brought together two kinds of dualisms, one inherited from apocalyptic Judaism and the other from Hellenistic philosophy. The apocalyptic dualism divided the messianic people of the new age from a fallen and apostate history. The Qumran community, for example, saw themselves as the messianic Israel of the age to come, over against the apostate temple and unconverted Jewish nation.[13]

In the Hellenistic Jewish philosopher Philo we see an exegesis built on the dualisms of letter and spirit, outwardness and inwardness, body and soul. Philo himself did not translate this into a sectarian type of Judaism; rather, he wished to give a sacramental understanding of Jewish laws and rites whereby the outward observances point to higher spiritual and universal truths. He did not negate the laws and rites themselves, but rather enjoined fellow Jews to observe them with a new understanding.[14]

The apocalyptic dualism of the messianic community and the apostate Israel fostered polemical sectarianism. In the Dead Sea Sect only the Qumran covenanters are regarded as the true Israel that will inherit the promises in the age to come. The apostate Israel will be cut off and thrown into the pit of fire. Yet the Qumran sect remained intra-Jewish. It sought to convert fellow Jews into its own community. Originally, Christianity probably shared this type of Jewish messianic sectarian perspective. But, as it became progressively Gentile and alienated from fellow Jews, it translated this intra-Jewish sectarianism into an anti-Jewish sectarianism. Judaism became the alien religion and nation that has been superseded and negated by God.

The absorption of the Platonic dualism of letter and spirit into the sectarian apocalyptic dualism allowed Christianity to define itself over against the old law and covenant. The old covenant and law is seen as only the 'fleshly foreshadowing' of a redemptive truth which is now fulfilled on a higher spiritual plane in Christianity. Christianity is seen as superseding Judaism, not only historically, but morally and even metaphysically. Judaism becomes only letter, fleshliness and carnality, over against Christianity as spirit and grace.[15]

The fallacy here lies in confusing the break between two historical peoples with the theological line between history and eschatology. The distinction between ambiguous historical existence and perfected messianic life is imported into history to define the line between two peoples and two historical eras. Israel as the harlot people (which, in the Old Testament, expressed critical historical realism) is used by Christianity to depict the Jews only in negative terms over against the perfectionist version of the church as the messianic bride of Christ. This results in a mystification of Christian reality. Christians project the shadow side of human life on to the Jews as the symbol of the fallen and unfulfilled side of human existence. We find here a polarization of two sides of a dialectic, which makes sense when applied to one community, but creates a completely distorted perspective, both for oneself and for the others, when split into two peoples and two 'eras'.

Judaism is not only 'letter', any more than Christianity is only 'spirit'. All religions, indeed all human cultures, are a complex dialectic of letter and spirit, faith and law. Religious renewal always wishes to make the content, the inner experience, predominant. But this never takes place without mediating community structures, patterns of prayer, creed, liturgy, ethics and community life. Christianity has certainly not been without all these embodiments. Indeed, ironically, its constant search for renewal of the inward experience means that it has proliferated far more 'embodiments' of itself than any other historical religion. But it has also mystified the relationship between the spirit and the institutional embodiments, either trying to deny historical embodiments, as in charismatic movements, or else idolizing its historical, institutional form as perfect and divinely given. Christians have yet to develop a realistic account of the relative, yet necessary relationship, between inward content and historical embodiment.

Christian churches have also tended to proliferate the supersessionist view of historical relationships. Not only is Christianity seen as superseding Judaism, but each renewed church sees itself as superseding its parent church. The new church is the true church of spirit and faith over the old church of dead letter and rote ritual. This same supersessionist pattern has also been projected into the secular doctrine of progress. 'Progressive' peoples see themselves as superseding and rendering obsolete 'unprogressive' peoples. We must criticize this supersessionist view of historical relationships between groups.

We can indeed value and affirm those breakthrough experiences of human life that allow new groups to arise and to develop new historical identities that are authentic and fulfilling. But this does not mean that the religion or nation from which this group has departed becomes superseded in some absolute way. They may be discovering, at that very same time, a way of renewing themselves on the basis of their traditional symbols and forms that is equally authentic.[16] Thus at the very period when it was shaking the dust of Judaism off its sandals, Christianity failed to notice that Judaism was undergoing a creative renewal. Indeed it was the Pharisees who refounded Judaism after the demise of the temple and laid the basis of rabbinic Judaism.

Christianity, as much as Judaism, continues to live in a dialectic of fulfilment and unfulfilment. Christianity, in the resurrection, looks back to a foundational experience that expresses hope and conquest

41

of defeat. Judaism, which did not participate in this particular experience, continues to renew itself out of the experience of the exodus, which mediates much the same message. For each, the hope mediated by the breakthrough experiences of liberation is the basis for a continued struggle for the final resolution to the riddle of history that is as much ahead of us Christians as it is ahead of the Jews.

The supersessionary pattern of Christian faith distorts both Jewish and Christian reality. We should rather think of Judaism and Christianity as parallel paths, flowing from common memories in Hebrew scripture, which are then reformulated into separate ways that lead two peoples to formulate the dialectic of past and future through different historical experiences. But the dilemma of foretaste and hope remains the same for both. For both live in the same reality of incompleted human existence itself.

4. *The key issue: christology*

The anti-Judaic patterns of Christian theology were and are still today tied to a dogma of fulfilled messianism. So it is not possible to rethink these anti-Judaic patterns without questioning its christological basis. There are two steps in this critique of christology which are necessary. First, Christians must formulate the faith in Jesus as the Christ in terms which are proleptic and anticipatory, rather than final and fulfilled. Jesus should not be said to fulfil all the Jewish hopes for the coming Messiah, which indeed he did not. Rather, he must be seen as one who announced this messianic hope and who gave signs of its presence, but who also died in that hope, crucified on the cross of unredeemed human history.

In his name we continue to proclaim that hope, and also to begin to experience its presence. But, like Jesus, we also do that under the cross of unresolved human contradictions. The final point of reference for the messianic advent still remains in the future. Its unambiguous arrival still eludes us. Here and now we, as much as the Jews, struggle with unresolved history, holding on to the memory of Jesus' resurrection from the cross as the basis for *our* refusal to take evil as the last word and *our* hope that God will win in the end.

This proleptic understanding of Jesus' messianic identity is familiar to Christian exegetes.[17] It has been particularly renewed in

42

liberation theologies. It is the exegesis that best translates the New Testament experience. Jesus' message is falsified when it is translated into a final fulfilment that is spiritualized and institutionally lodged in the past.

Secondly, we must see christology, not only as proleptic, but also as paradigmatic. We must accept its relativity to a particular people. This will be a more difficult principle for many Christians to accept, but it is equally inescapable. The cross and the resurrection are contextual to a particular historical community. These are breakthrough experiences which found *our* people, that mediate hope in the midst of adversity *for us*. But this does not mean that these are the only ways that this may happen, or that other people may not continue parallel struggles on different grounds; namely, the Jews, for whom the events in Jesus did not become paradigmatic events, and who continue to found themselves on the Exodus and the Torah as the memory and the way.

Some Christians will see such contextualizing of the Christian symbols as totally unacceptable. For them, Jesus as the only name that may be named on earth and in heaven is absolute. I can only say that our two thousand years of human experience do not allow that assertion to be taken literally. He may indeed be the only name *for us*. But other names continued to be named and do not fail to bear fruit. Nor does it seem to me that the power of Jesus' name will become less if we cease to use that name to deny the validity of other people's experience of God through other means. Indeed only when we cease to use Jesus' name to negate other peoples' experiences of the victory of life over death, can the name of Jesus cease to be a name that creates alienation of Jew from Christian, Christian from non-Christian. Instead we can begin to find new possibilities of human solidarity in our differing ways of mediating hope in the midst of defeat.

IV

Christology and Feminism: Can a Male Saviour Save Women?

Christology has been the doctrine of the Christian tradition that has been most frequently used against women. Historically this anti-woman use of christology reached its clearest formulation in the high scholasticism of Thomas Aquinas. Aquinas argued that the male is the normative or generic sex of the human species. Only the male represents the fullness of human potential, whereas woman by nature is defective physically, morally and mentally. Not merely after the Fall, but in the original nature of things, woman's 'defective nature' confined her to a subservient position in the social order. She is by nature under subjugation. Therefore it follows that the incarnation of the Logos of God into the male is not a historical accident, but an ontological necessity. The male represents wholeness of human nature, both in himself and as head of the woman. He is the fullness of the image of God, whereas woman by herself does not represent the image of God and does not possess wholeness of humanity.[1] This view of the male generic character of the *imago dei* is also found in St Augustine.[2]

It follows for Aquinas that woman cannot represent headship either in society or in the church. Her inability to be ordained follows from her defective or (as Aquinas put it, following Aristotle's biology) her 'misbegotten' nature. Just as Christ had to be incarnated in the male, so only the male can represent Christ. Mary Daly's succinct judgment in her book, *Beyond God the Father*, would seem to be fully vindicated in Aquinas' theology: 'When God is male, the male is God.'[3]

This male-dominant theology, that relegates woman to inferior status in both creation and redemption, has enjoyed considerable

45

revival in recent years as the keystone of the conservative reaction to the movements for women's ordination. In Roman Catholic, Anglican and Orthodox writings against women's ordination a certain constellation of arguments emerges, centred in the relation of maleness, christology and priesthood.[4] Jesus' historical example is usually cited. Jesus appointed no women disciples; therefore he desired no women to be ordained (without recognition of the historical gaps and anachronisms of this argument).

But the matter is deeper than historical example. This is no issue of passing and relative social forms. No emergence of women as equal to men in society can change the context of the discussion. For these writers, the exclusion of women from church leadership is not based on particular structures of society. Even the traditional doctrine of order of nature is left to the side. Rather, the neo-conservatives wish to see in the exclusion of women some unchangeable sacramental 'mystery' that links the maleness of the priest with the maleness of Christ. The bridegroom-bride symbolism is seen as central to this argument. Christ as the head and bridegroom of the church must necessarily be male, and, hence, also his representative, the priest. Obviously only males can be bridegrooms, although, oddly enough, these writers find no difficulty in the idea that males, in the laity, are 'brides'. It is taken for granted that this symbol system of bridegroom over bride, as head over body, male over female, is a revealed truth, rather than itself being simply a projection of a certain male-dominated social order.

Behind this christological argument of the necessary maleness of Christ and his representative, the priest, lies, it seems to me, a theological assumption; namely, the maleness of God. Not just Jesus' historical humanity, but the divine Logos, the disclosure of the 'Father', is necessarily male. In a remarkable forgetfulness of their own traditions of analogy and the *via negativa*, images such as 'Father' and 'Son' for God are not regarded as partial images drawn from limited (male) human experience, but are taken literally. 'Daughter' or 'mother' are not regarded as equally appropriate analogies.

The disclosure of God in history is seen as a disclosure of a fundamentally male reality in such a way as to exclude women from representing this divine redemptive action. They can only represent the passive, the receptive, never the active side of the divine disclosure. The Vatican Declaration against the Ordination of Women in 1976 sums up this new theological materialism when it declares that there must be a 'physical resemblance' between the priest and Christ.[5] Since this strange new version of the imitation of Christ does not exclude a Negro, a Chinese or a Dutchman from representing a first-century Jew, or a wealthy prelate from representing a carpenter's son, or sinners from representing the saviour, we must assume this imitation of Christ has now been reduced to one essential element, namely, male sex.

Numerous leading Roman Catholic theologians, including Karl Rähner, have actually condemned this Declaration as 'heretical' at this point.[6] That the Vatican would have unleashed such a document as an authoritative statement seems to me very significant. It reveals the extent of the contradiction between the message of Jesus as redeemer of all humanity 'in which there is neither male nor female' (Gal. 3.28), and the construction of christology through symbols that make it the instrument of patriarchal domination. The question I wish to ask in this chapter is: can christology be liberated from its encapsulation in the structures of patriarchy and really become an expression of liberation of women? Or is it so linked with symbols of male-dominance that it is unredeemable as good news for women?

Certainly many feminists have already concluded that the maleness of Christ is so fundamental to Christianity that women cannot see themselves as liberated through him. Thinkers such as Mary Daly or members of the Women's Spirituality Movement have already declared that women must reject Christ as redeemer for women and seek instead a female divinity and messianic symbol.[7] Thus the question of whether a male saviour can save women is not merely a provocative theoretical question. It is one on which many thousands of women have already voted with their feet by leaving the church and seeking alternative feminist communities.

I will look at three alternative models of christology to see whether there are other resources in the Christ symbol that might disclose different options from those discussed above. These are *(a)* the imperial Christ; *(b)* the androgynous Christ; and *(c)* the prophetic, iconoclastic Christ.

(a) The imperial Christ

The imperial Christ of Nicene theology was constructed by the fusion of two basic symbols from the twin heritages of Christian theology: Hebrew messianism and Greek philosophy. The Messiah symbol was drawn from Hebrew sacral kingship. In the Zechariah prophecy this Messiah is described as a warrior-king who will over-throw enemy empires and install Israel, the oppressed nation, in power. The enemy nations will be reduced to client states who will come up to Jerusalem to pay tribute to the new imperial ruling centre of the world.[8] This vision represents the dream of revenge of the oppressed nation which will, through God's help, turn the tables on the great imperial nations, and itself become the new imperial ruling power.

To this dream of the messianic ruler of the new age, Greek philosophy added the concept of the divine Logos or Nous of God which discloses the mind of God and manifests, in noetic form, the plan of nature. This Nous of God is not only *demiourgos*, or agent of God in creation, but also the means through which the universe is governed. This concept is set in the context of a hierarchical 'chain of Being'. Just as the Nous of God governs nature, so the Greeks must govern barbarians, masters govern slaves and men govern women. The free Greek male is seen as the natural aristocrat, representing mind and headship in nature. Women, slaves and barbarians are the 'body people' who must be governed, who are 'servile by nature'.[9] Greek political thought in the Hellenistic period linked this Logos theology with the universal emperor who must act in the body politic as the representative of the Nous of God govern-ing the universe.[10]

In the christology of Eusebius of Caesarea, adviser to Constantine at the Nicene Council in AD 325, these two heritages of Hebrew messianism and Greek Logos philosophy are brought together. Christ becomes the Pantocrator, the cosmic governor of a new Christianized universal empire. The Christian emperor, with the Christian bishop at his right hand, becomes the new Vicar of Christ on earth, governing the Christian state of the new redeemed order of history.[11] In this vision, patriarchy, hierarchy, slavery, and

48

Graeco-Roman imperialism have all been taken over and baptized by the Christian church.

Needless to say, elements of this christology might have been constructed in a different way. The victory of the Messiah as vindicator of the oppressed might have been seen as the radical levelling of all hierarchy and subjugation rather than the installation of the New Israel as the centre of a new empire. The Hebrew counterpart of the Logos doctrine identifies God's creative and redeeming Word as Holy Wisdom, represented as a female rather than male symbol.[12] But these options were lost in official Christian development. Instead, imperial christology wins in the fourth century as a sacralized vision of patriarchal, hierarchical and Euro-centred imperial control.

(b) Androgynous christologies

I would like to turn now to a number of alternative christologies that represent Christ as unifying male and female. I mention here gnostic christologies of the early Church, mediaeval Jesus mysticism, especially in Julian of Norwich, women Joachite leaders of the late Middle Ages, nineteenth-century Anglo-American sects, such as the Shakers, and finally Protestant pietism. All of these have been seen as marginal or heretical except pietism, which has actually become the dominant spirituality of much of Western Christianity in the bourgeois era. The root of these christologies lies in the basic Christian affirmation that Christ redeems the whole of human nature, male and female. In Paul's words, in Christ there is 'neither male nor female'.

These ideas are elaborated in the gnostic gospels. The Second Epistle of Clement states:

> For the Lord himself being asked by someone when his Kingdom would come, said: When the two shall be one, and the outside as the inside, the male with the female, neither male nor female.[13]

Christ is seen as the restored androgene of the original creation, before the separation of female from male. Women are seen as equal participants in this gnostic redeemed humanity, but only by abolishing their roles as sexual persons and mothers. The Gospel of the Egyptians has Jesus declare: 'I have come to destroy the works of the female', i.e. sexual desire and procreation (ch. 9.63), while the Gospel of Thomas vindicates the inclusion of women in redemption by having Jesus say, 'Lo, I shall lead her, and make her male, so that she too may become a living spirit resembling you males. For every woman who makes herself male will enter the Kingdom of Heaven' (Logion 114).[14]

Ancient gnostic androgyny, as well as its modern revivals in mystics, such as Jacob Boehme,[15] is androcentric. Maleness and femaleness are still seen as opposite principles standing for mind and spirit *versus* sense, body and sexuality. The two are brought together in a male-centred concept of the self in which the female is neutralized.

A somewhat different tradition is developed in the Jesus mysticism of Julian of Norwich. Here Jesus is declared to be both mother and father. Like a mother Jesus feeds us with his own body. He nurtures us first with milk, as newborn babes in the faith. The ambiance of these images of the mothering Jesus in mediaeval mysticism is found particularly in eucharistic piety. But since both the human and the divine person of Christ was firmly established in mediaeval thought as male, this means that mothering or female qualities are taken into the male. In Christ the male gains a mode of androgyny, of personhood that is both commanding and nurturing. But it is doubtful that Julian's society would have allowed her to reverse the relation and give to women, through Christ, the right to exercise the male prerogatives.[16]

Perhaps the boldest effort to bring the female into redemption is found in a couple of little-known female leaders of sectarian movements in the tradition of Joachim of Fiore. The Joachimites believed that the Second Age of the Son, represented by the clerical church, would be superseded by a Third Age of the Spirit, which would bring redemption to perfection. This notion allowed many dissatisfied groups in the late mediaeval world to express their disaffiliation with the existing ecclesiastical and feudal hierarchies. Most Joachimites did not see the vindication of the female as a part of their agenda. But one such group gathered around Prous Boneta, founder of a Provencal Beguin sect. They believed she was the incarnation of the Holy Spirit, the new Eve who would bring final salvation to all humanity.[17]

Another group in Milan declared that their leader, Guglielma, was the incarnate Spirit. Just as the second person of the Trinity had appeared as a male, so the new dispensation of the Spirit will appear as a female. The Guglielmites believed that all authority had departed from the corrupt hierarchy. In the new church, built on the foundations of the Spirit, there will be four new spiritual gospels, and women will be spiritual leaders.[18] Such groups were marginal even with the sects, and were regarded by the church as monstrous heresies to be stamped out immediately. Yet here we have the stirring of a much more radical dissatisfaction. Here women do not merely affirm a mothering or female element within a male-centred symbol, but dare to dream of turning the tables on the male-dominated world. Only in recent years, in the feminist Goddess movements, have we seen similar ideas where women announce a 'return of the Goddess', signalling better humanity that will supersede the corrupt religion mediated through the male redeemer.

Although feminist Joachimites were exterminated in the Middle Ages, it is probable that ideas of this kind continued to gestate from various sources in underground currents of European sectarian and mystical thought. Otherwise it is hard to explain the appearance in the late eighteenth century in England of a Quaker sect called the Shakers who also declared their faith in a female Messiah who would supersede and complete the redemption through Jesus.

The Shakers based their belief in a dual Christ, both male and female, on their doctrine of God. God is androgynous, both Father and Mother. So the incarnation of God must take place in both the male and female forms. Redemption has been incomplete so far because it has taken place only in male form. However, in their founder, Mother Ann Lee, the Shakers believed that the long-awaited female Messiah, the manifestation of divine wisdom, had at last appeared, completing the salvation of humanity.[19] This parity of male and female in redeemed humanity must also be expressed in a parity of male and female leaders in the messianic community. However, the Shakers followed the gnostic tradition in defining this messianic community as celibate.

The idea of a need for a new dispensation in female form enjoyed wide currency in the nineteenth century. It is found in such diverse sources as the French utopian socialists, the St Simonians,[20] and the New England Transcendentalists. It is constantly hinted at in Mary

51

Baker Eddy's new Church of Christian Science, who even declared that since the highest meaning of God is Love, the 'feminine' nature is closer to God than the masculine.[21] Eddy rewrote the Lord's Prayer to read: 'Our Mother-Father God'.

These movements reflect widespread unrest in nineteenth-century thought over male and female identities in relation to religion and society. Underlying this unrest are shifting political and economic patterns. The secular liberal revolutions displaced religion from the public political order and located religion instead in the private sphere. At the same time industrialization was depriving women in the home of many of their traditional productive functions. Poor women were being drawn out of the home into the factory. But the normative nature of woman was being redefined in terms of the bourgeois housewife, who was primarily seen as a nurturer, rather than a productive labourer in a family business.

This new role of the bourgeois wife coalesced with the privatization of religion to unite the definition of Christianity with the definition of womanliness. This accorded with a pietist tradition that defined religion in terms of affect or feeling, rather than reason or dogma. Woman was seen as the more natural bearer of the Christlike virtues of love, altruism and self-sacrifice. Spirituality, piety and self-abnegation were seen as particularly appropriate for women (i.e. 'good' domesticated women).

This idea of women as more Christlike than men allowed very different interpretations that raged on both sides of the battle over women's emancipation in nineteenth-century America. For conservatives, woman's sweetness and goodness was fragile and can be preserved only by the strictest segregation in the home and renunciation of all desires for education, influence or leadership. For many feminists, on the other hand, this notion of woman's Christlike nature suggested a messianic meaning to the emergence of woman. If woman represents the higher human qualities of peace, purity, reconciliation and love, then these qualities are too good to keep at home. These are just what the world needs to save it from the various evils that corrupt society. The home, in nineteeth-century female reformism, becomes the launching pad for a crusade into society to redeem it and elevate it to the female standards of goodness.

These traditions of the androgynous Christ reveal an ambivalent heritage. All exhibit a sense that a masculinist Christ is inadequate to express full human redemption, that Christ must in some way represent both male and female. The earlier tradition sees the female as the lower element to be united into the higher male element. But, as we move into the nineteenth century, the valuation shifts. The female comes to be seen as the 'better half', representing redemptive qualities that will uplift and perfect humanity. The emergence of woman points to a messianic future that will transform the male world of war, conflict and exploitation into the woman's world of peace and reconciliation.

This heritage still divides the woman's movement today. Women can't decide whether they want to 'get into the man's world', defined as an evil world, but also the 'real world', or hold out for a better but non-existent (utopian) world represented by the still unempowered 'feminine' principles.

(c) The prophetic iconoclastic Christ

Another perspective on christology is being elaborated by liberation theologies. Liberation theologies go back to nineteenth century movements of Christian socialism that began to seek alliances between the gospel and the Left. Liberation theologies base their christologies particularly on the Jesus of the synoptic gospels. Here is a Jesus who does not sacralize existing ruling classes. The messianic prophet proclaims his message as an iconoclastic critique of existing élites, particularly religious élites. The gospel drama is one of prolonged conflict between Christ and those religious authorities who gain their social status from systems of ritualized righteousness. Jesus proclaims an iconoclastic reversal of this system of religious status. The leaders of the religious establishment are blind guides and hypocrites, while the outcasts of the society, socially and morally, prostitutes, publicans, Samaritans, are able to hear the message of the prophet. In Matthew's language, 'Truly the tax collectors and the harlots go into the kingdom of God before you', i.e., the scribes and Pharisees (Matt. 21.31). The gospel turns upside down the present order; the first shall be last and the last first.

This reversal of order is not simply a turning upside down of the present hierarchy, but aims at a new order where hierarchy itself is overcome as a principle of rule. This may have been the source of the messianic struggle between Jesus and his own disciples. It certainly has been the root of misunderstanding of Jesus by the church historically. When the sons of Zebedee ask Jesus if they can sit on his left and right hands when he comes into his Kingdom, he confronts them with his different vision of the way into the messianic future.

> You know that the rulers of the Gentiles lord it over them, and their great men exercise authority over them. It shall not be so among you; but whoever would be great among you must be your servant, and whoever would be first among you must be your slave; even as the Son of man came not to be served but to serve and to give his life as a ransom for many. (Matt. 20.25-27)

The meaning of servanthood in this oft-quoted and oft-misused text of Jesus cannot be understood either as a sacralized Christian lordship that calls itself 'servant', but reproduces the same characteristics of domination, or as the romanticizing of servitude. This is why neither existing lords nor existing servants can serve as a model for this servanthood, but only the Christ, the messianic person, who represents a new kind of humanity. The essence of servanthood is that it is possible only for liberated persons, not people in servitude. Also it exercises power and leadership, but in a new way, not to reduce others to dependency, but to empower and liberate others.

This means, in the language of liberation theology, that God as liberator acts in history to liberate all through opting for the poor and the oppressed of the present system. The poor, the downcast, those who hunger and thirst, have a certain priority in God's work of redemption. Part of the signs of the kingdom is that the lame walk, the blind see, the captives are freed, the poor have the gospel preached to them. Christ goes particularly to the outcasts, and they, in turn, have a special affinity for the gospel. But the aim of this partiality is to create a new whole, to elevate the valleys and make the high places low, so that all may come into a new place of God's reign, when God's will is done on earth.

How does the question of the subjugation and emancipation of women fit into such a vision of the iconoclastic prophetic Christ? This world view is not concerned with the dualism of male and female, either as total groups or as representatives of some cosmic principles that need to be related to each other. But women are not ignored in this vision. Indeed, if one can say that Christ comes to the oppressed and the oppressed especially hear him, then it is women within these marginal groups who are often seen both as the oppressed of the oppressed and also as those particularly receptive to the gospel. The dialogue at the well takes place not just with a Samaritan, but with a Samaritan woman. Not just a Syro-Phoenician, but a Syro-Phoenician woman is the prophetic seeker who forces Jesus to concede redemption to the non-Jews. Among the poor it is widows who are the exemplars of the most destitute; among the moral outcasts it is the prostitutes who represent the bottom of the list. This is not accidental. It means that, in the iconoclastic messianic vision, it is the women of the despised and outcast peoples who are seen as the bottom of the present hierarchy and hence, in a special way, the last who shall be first in the kingdom.

How does this vision of the redemptive work of Christ, that addresses itself particularly to the women among the outcast, differ from those messianic visions of the new age of the 'feminine' which we described earlier? It seems to me that it has some affinities with them, in the sense that Christ is seen as critic rather than vindicator of the present hierarchical social order. The meaning of Christ is located in a new future order still to come that transcends the power structures of historical societies, including those erected in the Christian era in 'Christ's name'.

But this biblical vision also differs in important ways from the romantic vision of the advent of the new age of the feminine. These gnostic and romantic traditions abstract the human person as male and female into a dualism of opposite principles, masculinity and femininity. They give different valuations to each side and then try to set up a scheme to unite the two in a new whole. This sets up an insoluble problem for human personhood until these qualities labelled masculine and feminine are seen as the product of social power relations rather than 'nature'. 'Woman-as-body-sensuality' and 'woman-as-pure-altruistic-love' are both abstractions of human potential created when one group of people in power is able to define other groups of people over against themselves. To abstract these definitions into eternal essences is to miss the social context in which these definitions arise.

The world of the gospels returns us to concrete social conditions in which maleness and femaleness are elements of a complex web in which humans have defined status, superiority and inferiority. The gospel returns us to the world of Pharisees and priests, widows and prostitutes, homeless Jewish prophets and Syro-Phoenician women. Men and women interact with each other within a multiplicity of social definitions: sexual status, but also ethnicity, social class, religious office and law define relations with each other. Jesus as liberator calls for a renunciation and dissolution of this web of status relationships by which societies have defined privilege and unprivilege. He speaks especially to outcast women, not as representatives of the 'feminine', but because they are at the bottom of this network of oppression. His ability to be liberator does not reside in his maleness, but, on the contrary, in the fact that he has renounced this system of domination and seeks to embody in his person the new humanity of service and mutual empowerment.

Together, Jesus and the Syro-Phoenician woman, the widow and the prostitute, not as male and female principles, but as persons responding authentically to each other, point us to that new humanity of the future. This new humanity is described in simple and earthy terms by Jesus as the time when 'all receive their daily bread, when each remits the debts which the others owe to them, when we are not led into temptations (including messianic temptations) but are delivered from evil'.

V

Ecology and Human Liberation: A Conflict between the Theology of History and the Theology of Nature?

Since the late 1960s there has been increasing attention in advanced industrial countries to the problem of 'ecology'. We have been told that the present patterns of industrialization and its postulate of endlessly expanding growth must be stopped or reversed. The basic fossil fuels, metals and minerals on which this indusrialization has been based are limited and running out. Therefore there is no possibility of expanding this pattern of development to (so-called) under-developed countries. Moreover, the side-effects of this industrialization are producing increasing amounts of toxic wastes that pollute the air, waters and soil and thus threaten the biosphere upon which human life is based. Finally, that population is outgrowing all possible growth in food production and the human race is faced with spreading famine. There must be systematic campaigns of birth control, particularly in Third World countries.

Without in any way disputing the critical nature of this situation, I wish to point out the danger of analysing these 'facts' solely in the context of the governments and intelligentsia of advanced industrial countries. This lens of analysis is characteristically myopic. For example, the 'population problem' is seen primarily as a problem of too many poor people, as though it is they who are causing overpopulation and famine.[1] This ignores the fact that many poor countries have a low population, in the sense of people per square mile, while affluent countries may also have high population density. Obviously there are other factors in chronic poverty and hunger than population density.

The pollution problem is seen primarily in terms of certain technological 'fixes' and clean-up programmes. It is assumed that this problem can be solved with better safety measures and new technology. But these regulations become mired in political subterfuge in which the regulators and producers of pollution-control devices are hand in glove with those who are causing the pollution.[2]

The question of scarce resources is viewed through several lenses. It is seen as part of an international struggle in which 'greedy' Arabs hold the rest of the world at ransom for their oil. It is also seen as a question of personal conservation in which the consumers of oil for petrol and heating must cut down their use and pay high prices. There is also a call for the development of alternative energy sources, such as solar energy, but we are told that the technology for this is not yet available for mass production.[3]

What is missed in all this type of analysis and response is a recognition that the ecological crisis has something to do with social domination. This crisis has its genesis in certain structures of power and ownership through which the project of industrialization has been pursued nationally and internationally. The exploitation of natural resources does not take place in an unmediated way. It takes place through the domination of labour which, in turn, necessitates the domination of the bodies of some people by other people. The abuse of the resources of the earth becomes acute when a small ruling class, who establish ownership and control of land, people and techniques, can use the labour of the vast majority of people to extract these resources, but without having to take into consideration their rights and needs as human persons.[4]

Exploitation of labour happens on many levels, from outright slave labour of blacks in South Africa or in the Western plantations of earlier European colonialism, to the peonage of Indians and peasants and the exploitative wage labour of industrial workers. The operating assumption of such a pattern of industrialization through social domination is that profits must be maximized for the owners. This is done not only by sharing as few of the benefits of this wealth as possible with those who work, but also by passing on the ecological costs of development to society at large, particularly in those regions where powerless people live. The workers will live in crowded tenements with chronic social problems, smokey skies and undrinkable water, while the owners will set themselves apart behind high walls in suburban estates with sparkling pools and green lawns. Indeed the 'ecological' question only really becomes a public question at all when it becomes increasingly difficult for, at least, the middle-management sectors of the affluent classes to set themselves and their families apart from the environmental and social costs of exploitation which had always been passed on to the poor from the very beginning of industrialization. The affluent classes seek to solve these problems without in any way challenging or changing the system of social domination that is its underlying presupposition.

Social domination is the missing link in the question of domination of nature. The environmental crisis is basically insoluble as long as a system of social domination remains intact that allows the owners and decision-makers to maintain high profits for the few by passing on the costs to the many in the form of low wages, high prices, bad working conditions and toxic side effects of the techniques of extraction.

(a) Theological patterns of 'man' and nature

It has been recognized that this ecological crisis which has caught up with Western civilization has a theological basis. Specifically it is said that the Judaeo-Christian tradition favoured a theory of subordination of nature and 'man's' domination over it. 'Be fruitful and multiply, and fill the earth and subdue it; and have dominion over the fish of the sea and over the birds of the air and over every living thing that moves on the face of the earth' (Gen. 1.28) is the biblical command. Today we have to question not only the fertility ethic, but also the ethic of unrestricted domination over the rest of creation. If dominion over nature means unrestricted rights to pollute and destroy, then it is self-defeating. Since humanity is tied inextricably to interdependence with plants, animals, water, soil and air, the health and prosperity of the human community is not possible without the health of the non-human community which encompasses us. Thus ecologists have argued for a new theology and ethic of nature based on mutuality and interdependence rather than domination and subordination.

However, this question of a new ethic of 'man' and 'nature' is misleading. We cannot assume that humans as a whole have adopted and profited from any such concepts of domination of nature. Or that the crisis can be resolved by adopting a new personal ethic and world view of symbiosis and enjoyment of nature. An ecological ethic cannot stop at protection of parks and rivers for wilderness hiking and camping for the leisured classes! We must recognize the hidden message of social domination that lies within the theological and ideological traditions of domination of nature. 'Man's' domination of nature has never meant humans in general, but ruling-class males. The hidden link in their domination of nature has always been the dominated bodies, the dominated labour of women, slaves, peasants and workers. It is not surprising, then, that it is these dominated persons who are seen as 'closer' to nature, more a part of nature, partaking more of the bodily and sensual 'nature' than ruling-class males, who view themselves as having a higher intellectual nature, being closer to mind and spirit and, ultimately, closer to God than these dominated 'nature-people'.

This connection of subordination of nature and social domination is very evident in the language of classical patriarchy inherited from Hebrew Law and Greek philosophy. In Hebrew Law, God is seen as a great patriarch who creates the world as 'his' handicraft and rules over it as a sovereign master. The human community, Israel, has been chosen by him. Israel is his wife or daughter, his sons, his servants. Thus the language for the God-human community is drawn from the language of patriarchal domination over the subordinate persons in the family: wives, children, slaves or servants. The law code is addressed, not to Israel as a whole, but to the patriarchal class, the male heads of families. Children, slaves and wives are viewed both as dependents and as species of property that can be used and disposed of in various ways.[5]

In Greek philosophy the world is viewed as a hierarchy of mind over body, a noumenal world of spirit over a phenomenal world of material existence. This not only divides the individual into a dualism in which the ruling mind is seen as engaged in struggle to subdue a recalcitrant body, but it also divides society into the same dualism. According to Aristotle's *Politics*, ruling-class Greek males are the natural exemplars of mind or reason, while women, slaves and barbarians are the naturally servile people who must be subdued and ruled by their 'head'.[6] Plato also, in the *Republic*, divides society into three classes, along what is presumed to be the division of the self into mind, passions and appetites. These correspond to the three classes of society; the philosophers, the warriors and the peasants and workers.

Although Plato includes women in all three classes, he also assumes that women will be less skilled than men in all three classes.[7] In the *Timaeus*, when Plato tells us that when the incarnate soul loses its struggle against the passions and appetites, it is incarnated into a woman and then into an animal,[8] we see clearly that the hierarchy of 'man' over nature, mind over body, presupposes the hierarchy of 'head-people' over 'body-people'. Women, whose bodies mediate physical existence to humanity, become the oldest archetype of this connection between social domination and domination of nature. This is why nature is symbolized as female; the domination of nature as the domination of a wife and the exploitation of nature as the 'rape' of a woman. These metaphors of spirit over nature, mind over body, as male over female, master over slave, also sanction the hierarchies of social domination. They are made to appear to be 'natural'; not as social constructs but as the givens of a necessary and divinely-created order of things.

The patriarchal view of nature as dominated body supposed that nature could be good and serviceable if it could be reduced to compliant obedience. But lurking underneath this project of domination of body was the fear of the revolt of the body. The body was seen as subversive, threatening to 'drag the manly mind down from its heavenly heights to wallow in the flesh', to quote St Augustine.[9] The sensuality of servile people, women and slaves, was seen as debasing the spirit. Underneath this fear of embodiment as moral debasement lies the fear of death. The ruling mind seeks to sever its connections with biological existence altogether, to imagine that it originated in an incorruptible realm of eternal life, whence it has accidentally, or through some mysterious fault, fallen into this embodied form. The domination of the body, nature and woman turns into a flight from the body, nature and woman. For at least 1300 years Western civilization became obsessed with this world-fleeing agenda and shaped its ethics, religion and cultural institutions around it.

Flight from the body partly contradicts the patriarchal project of social domination. Women are declared to be freed from the burdens of sex and reproduction to share as equals in this flight from the world.[10] Social classes are said to have become equal. Those who flee the world give up social privilege and wealth and embrace voluntary poverty. Following Jesus, they sell what they have and give to the poor.

But the ascetic movement originated primarily in alienated members of the ruling classes and continued to be based sociologically in these classes. The ascetic leaders of the fourth century and the early Middle Ages were members of noble and princely classes and established their places of retreat upon their landed estates. Abbots and abbeys soon became integrated into the system of feudal nobility and landed power. Monks and nuns ceased to do their own work and became rulers of vast mansions and estates of toiling servants and serfs.[11] It became difficult, if not impossible, for poor people to join monasteries.

In the later Middle Ages, revolts of the urban classes created subversive monastic movements in which voluntary poverty became an attack on the wealth of the mighty. This is found in the left-wing or spiritual Franciscans, as well as Joachimite radicals, Beguines and other later mediaeval popular movements.[12] But, by and large, the flight from body and nature continued to be based upon social domination and supported it, while at the same time being the compensation for its bad conscience.

The rational and systematic application of technique to the control of nature was pioneered by monastic orders. The Cistercians became the agricultural pioneers of the Middle Ages, expanding and subduing the uncleared wildernesses of Europe.[13] The Franciscan scholastics led in the application of speculative science to technique. But as culture and the economy began to recover, the project of flight from nature became contradictory to the new possibilities of domination of nature that were emerging. Asceticism imbued mediaeval Europe with a fear of nature, the body and woman as demonic. Fallen nature was the realm of the Devil. Those who ventured too deeply into 'her' mysterious secrets or went out exploring uncharted lands and seas were likely to encounter demonic spirits.

The early scientists were always in danger of being accused of having sold their souls to the Devil in order to learn the secrets of mastery of nature.[14] Outbreaks of disorder in society or nature were believed to be fomented by secret agents of the Devil in the form of witches, old peasant women who had sold themselves to the Devil.

These fears of demonic bodiliness and social disorder erupted in the late Mediaeval and Reformation periods in prolonged bouts of witch-hunting which took the lives of as much as a million people, most of them women.[15]

Gradually Europe began to revolt against other-worldliness. The Reformation, the Renaissance, the Scientific Revolution and the Enlightenment all pointed back to this world as 'man's' true home. Philosophy and science begin what might be called the 'exorcism' of nature, and religion gradually catches up. The devils are driven out of the material world, and it is redeemed as a realm for human knowledge and exploitation. This brings a new celebration of nature, its beauty, its order. Instead of the realm of the Devil, it becomes the immanence of God, exhibiting in its regularity the indwelling divine Reason. It is the rationality of nature that is celebrated by these Enlightenment thinkers. Because of its rationality, nature is intrinsically knowable by 'man', reducible to mathematical formulas which, in turn, become the key to mastery and rule over nature.[16]

In Descartes we have a new appearance of the dualism of mind and body. The mind as knower of nature is seen as transcendent and separated from the object of knowledge. Nature as object of knowledge is reduced to 'dead matter' operating according to fixed rules that can be known and applied to increasing control over the 'machine' of nature.[17] A new priesthood of scientists arises hand in hand with the new entrepreneurial masters of the expanding world of European capitalism and colonialism.[18] To the labour of women, peasants, workers and servants in Europe there are now added vast new lands to be subdued, vast new armies of bodies to be made the instruments of extractive labour. The foundations are laid for a new union of the domination of nature through social domination as a global system.

(b) Responses to scientific and industrial domination

As the allied powers of scientific technology, industrialization and colonialism began to work their transforming effects upon Europe and then America, certain responses appeared that partly supported and partly contradicted this project. We can summarize these as

(1) the liberal progressive response, (2) the Marxist revolutionary response, and (3) the romantic reaction.

(1) The liberal progressive response represents the ideology of the expanding bourgeois against the old feudal aristocracy. At first it sponsors new doctrines of civil freedom and social equality. Christian eschatology is incarnated back into history in the vision of infinitely expanding progress. Through science, applied in rational education and technology, the superstitions that have held humanity in bondage will be vanquished and an infinitely expanding progress will be opened up in which all the evils of ignorance, poverty, injustice and disease will be conquered. Visionaries like the Marquis de Condorcet see this triumphant progress expanding gradually to include all classes and races, and even women, in its emancipatory embrace.[19]

But this élan of progress was based on the domination of labour and material resources of the under-classes and the colonized empires. Soon the egalitarianism of the bourgeois against the old ruling classes of clergy and nobility gave way to a new classism and racism. It is said that power through progress is the special prerogative of a privileged class; a Euro-American Protestant male white ruling class has a divinely-given mandate to expand and subdue the earth and rule over it. The lesser peoples of the world, Catholic Celts and Southern Europeans, brown and black-skinned peoples, Jews, Arabs, Orientals; these are fated by their biological inferiority to fall by the wayside, either to be exterminated or integrated into the new civilization that will arise through the triumphant march of the divine Spirit through history. The underside of progress is the justification of the defeat of the victims of progress.[20]

Insofar as progressivism kept the liberal hopes of expanding justice and equality, it was through the expansion of its own system. Gradually the conquest of nature through science and technology would include everyone, even those impoverished masses of the Third World. The poverty and squalor of the colonized world is not recognized as the effects of colonization itself which exploited their resources through exploiting their labour. But, rather, it is regarded as a sign of their retardation, their failure to emerge into industrialization, which will be cured by further expansion of the same system of 'development'. Many Third World nations today are still pursuing this will-o'-the-wisp of Euro-American sponsored development and wondering why the chronic contradictions of their societies get worse all the time rather than better.[21]

(2) The Marxist revolutionary response is based on many of the same presuppositions as the liberal progressive ideology. It too envisages endlessly expanding material prosperity through the expansion of industrialization and technological domination of nature. Anti-spiritual scientism of the eighteenth century atheistic French Enlightenment continues to be its reigning dogma. But Marxism recognizes a basic truth unnoticed by liberal progressivism; namely, that the expanding power over nature has been based on social domination. So the continuing expansion of this system will not create increasing prosperity and equality for all, but rather increasing contradictions between the wealth of the few and the poverty of the many. A social revolution of ownership is necessary. At the critical moment, when the structure of industrialization has been fully constructed by the bourgeois, the workers will revolt, take over the productive machine and create a new society of justice, in which nature can be dominated without social domination.[22]

(3) Finally, there is the romantic reaction to the 'modern' world. A combination of poets, artists, and spokespersons for the feudal and peasant societies begin to recoil against the world of science and industrialization. These have different social agendas, which is what makes romanticism such a mass of contradictions. But basically romanticism suggests that urbanization, technological rationality and industrialization are alienating 'man' from his roots in 'nature'. 'Nature' is used here in a different way from the philosophy of science. It means the irrational, the intuitive, the organic over against rationalized machine culture.[23]

Return to nature for some means a return to a different way of knowing, using senses and feeling rather than rational abstraction. For others it means a return to the agrarian and handicraft village society that is being destroyed by the machine. For others it means a romanticized return to the feudal world of knights and ladies, folk mythology and Gothic architecture.

The people who were the victims of social domination now become idealized as special bearers of intuitive wisdom and 'harmony with nature'. Women, peasants, Indians and South Sea Islanders become the 'noble savages' of this quest by the male ruling class to overcome its sense of alienation and loss of roots. Ancient matriarchies and tribal communities are imagined once to have reigned over a lost paradise of spontaneous harmony of society with nature.[24] Salvation lies in a recovery of this nature-wisdom and a utopian reconstruction of this pre-industrial folk society.

Romanticism raised critical questions about alienation from nature and the need to seek societies of human scale and balance between the human and the natural world. The counter-cultural wing of the ecological movement continues to draw heavily upon the romantic utopian tradition, as do branches of feminism and the liberation of native tribal peoples.[25] But there are many dangers in the romantic consciousness. Originating in the alienation of a male ruling class from its own industrial world, it stereotypes the victims of this system as the guardians of all the opposite characteristics.

Romanticism fails to recognize this complementarity of male and female, West and East, North and South as the product of socialization, but raises it to the level of eternal cosmic archetypes.[26] It thus colonizes the exploited people anew by fashioning them into the rest and recreation spots for weary white males. Wives, Indians and South Sea Islanders are to be kept in their islands of natural tranquillity so they can nurture and restore to wholeness the alienated souls of affluent white males. The romantic project of return to nature becomes personalistic and escapist, rather than a real grappling with the interconnections of social and natural domination and an effort to reconstruct these relationships in a new way.

(c) Towards a new world view of eco-justice

It is evident that although each of these traditions has elements we would wish to affirm – the freedoms of the liberal tradition; the economic justice of the socialist tradition; the recovery of nature of the romantic tradition – we are far from being able to put them together in a coherent world view, much less of translating this into a guide for effective action. In the concluding part of this chapter I will suggest some outlines of such an ecological-libertarian world view.

First, the Western dream of infinitely expanding power and wealth defies the actual finitude of ourselves and the world and conceals the exploitative use of other people's resources. It must be replaced with a new culture of acceptance of finitude and limits. But not in the sense of a 'static-state' society which simply fixates the present poverty and inequality. We must *change,* not as endless growth, but as 'conversion'. Conversion means that we rediscover the finitude of the earth as a balance of elements, which together harmonize to support life for all parts of the community.

Conversion means the interconnectedness of all parts of the community of creation so that no part can long flourish if the other parts are being injured or destroyed. In a system of interdependence, no part is intrinsically 'higher' or 'lower'. Plants are not 'lower' than humans because they don't think or move. Rather, their photosynthesis is the vital process that underlies the very existence of the animal and human world. We could not exist without them, whereas they could exist very well without us. Who, then, is more 'important'?[27]

The hierarchical model of reality is misleading. Ecological harmony is based on diversity in which each part has an equally vital part to play in maintaining the renewed harmony and balance of the whole.[28] We must start thinking of reality as the connecting links of a dance in which each part is equally vital to the whole, rather than the linear competitive model in which the above prospers by defeating and suppressing what is below.[29]

The whole concept of control of nature through top-down domination is an illusion. There are only two real options, ecological balance or destructive imbalance which creates increasingly toxic side-effects. To dominate nature or other people in a way that is destructive to their welfare does not increase our 'control'. It may appear to do so for a while, but ultimately it creates increasingly uncontrollable morbidity which undermines everyone's survival. This is basically the state that the whole global system of life is moving towards at the present time. At the end, it will be the flies and roaches who will inherit the earth after the four horsemen of famine, pollution, disease and war have been unleashed.

A non-hierarchical world-view will also challenge many Western theological assumptions. We must question the cherished dualism between the Hebrew linear view of salvation history over against 'cyclical nature religions'. Modern Western biblical scholars have greatly exaggerated this dualism in the Bible. The Canaanite religious vision of recurrent renewal is not simply an immersion in bodily and seasonal processes. The victory of divinity over chaos implies social justice as well as natural prosperity.[30]

Hebrew thought took over this religion of renewal of nature and society, but it shifted its focus to history rather than seasonal recurrences. The struggle to restore justice in society and harmony with nature becomes a historical project that defines the fallenness and hope of humanity. For Hebrew thought there is one covenant of creation that includes nature and society. To break the covenant of creation is to create both social injustice and natural catastrophe. Whereas the restoration of the covenant of creation unites social harmony and peaceful, prosperous relations with nature. Natural disaster is no longer seen as simply a matter of capricious natural powers. It reflects social injustice. This Hebrew prophetic sense of the interconnection of harmony with nature and social justice is particularly important for the construction of an ethic of eco-justice.[31]

Finally, we must question the linear model of history that sees it moving, either in an evolutionary or revolutionary manner, to some final static end-point of salvation. This concept of a final salvific end-point of history is intrinsically contrary to created existence and leads to several contradictions. Either this end-point escapes outside history altogether and ceases to provide any hope, reducing all human history to 'one damn thing after another'. Or else it leads to the mythical pursuit of a revolution that can never come. If this final salvation is identified with any particular social revolution, it tends to absolutize this revolution and hence to make it totalitarian.

We need a fundamentally different model of human hope and change. I suggest conversion rather than either infinite growth or a final revolution. Conversion suggests that, although there is no one utopian system of humanity that lies back in a paradise of the past, there are certain ingredients of a just and liveable society. These include the human scale of habitats and communities; an ability of people to participate in the decisions that govern their lives; work in which everyone is able to integrate intelligence and creativity with manual labour; a certain just sharing of the profits and benefits of production; a balance of leisure and work, rural and urban environments. Most of us sense what the elements of this humanized life are like and are constantly trying to get back to it, often in our leisure time.

Perhaps instead of the eschatological end-point of history, we should take our model of messianic redemption from the Hebrew idea of the Jubilee (Lev. 25.8-12). The Jubilee teaches that there are certain basic elements that make for life as God intended it on earth. Everyone has their own vine and fig tree. No one is enslaved to another. The land and animals are not overworked. But human sinfulness tends to create a drift away from this intended state. Some people's land is expropriated by others. People are sold into bondage. Nature is overworked. So, on a periodic basis, there must be a revolutionary conversion. Unjust debts that have piled up over a long period of time must be liquidated. Those who are sold into slavery are released; the land that has been expropriated is returned. Land and animals are allowed rest. Humanity and nature recover their just balance.

This cannot be done once for all. To be human is to change as well as to die. Both change and death are good. They belong to the natural limits of human life. We must seek the life intended by God for us within these limits. The return to harmony in the covenant of creation is not a matter of cyclical return to the same, for each new achievement of workable balances is different, based on new environments and technologies. It is a historical project that has to be undertaken again and again in changing circumstances. Each great social movement, such as the labour movement, leaves some needed changes undone and generates new contradictions. So it is left for a new generation to undertake again the project of a just and viable life for their times.

This concept of social change as conversion back to the centre, rather than to a beginning or end-point in history, seems to me a model of change that is more in keeping with temporal existence, rather than subjecting us to the tyranny of impossible expectations. Jesus' own vision of the Kingdom as release of captives, remission of debts, provision of daily bread, has more to do with this Jubilee vision than with the apocalyptic doctrine of the end-point of history.[32] We need to recover the Hebrew sense of the mortal limits of covenantal existence, rather than the apocalyptic and Greek flight from mutability.

I suggest we think of the messianic hope to which Jesus points us, not as the eschatological end-point of history or as transcendence of death, but rather as the Shalom of God which remains the true connecting point of all our existences, even when we violate and forget it. Redemptive hope is the constant quest for that Shalom of

God which holds us all together, as the operative principle of our collective lives. God's Shalom is the nexus of authentic creational life that has to be reincarnated again and again in new ways and new contexts in each new generation.

NOTES

NOTES

I *Jesus and the Revolutionaries*

1. It is significant that the recent Vatican investigations of Hans Küng and Edward Schillebeeckx focus on christology. Vatican investigations of Latin American theologians, such as Leonardo Boff and Jon Sobrino, also see christology as the critical issue. The concern with christology in these disputes between the Vatican *magisterium* and critical theologians is closely correlated with a certain model of church polity. The *magisterium* is basically concerned to defend its own legitimacy as 'founded' by Jesus. Historical views of Jesus that see him as an iconoclastic prophetic figure within Judaism threaten this model of the historical foundation of the Roman *magisterium* in the intentionality of Jesus!

2. Pinchas, *Ist das nicht Josephs Sohn? Jesus im heutigen Judentum*, Calwer Verlag, Stuttgart 1976. The English title is in fact *Israelis, Jews and Jesus*, Doubleday, New York 1979.

3. S.G.F. Brandon, *The Fall of Jerusalem and the Christian Church*, SPCK 1951.

4. S.G.F. Brandon, *Jesus and the Zealots*, Manchester University Press 1967.

5. S.G.F. Brandon, *The Trial of Jesus*, Batsford and Stein and Day, New York 1968.

6. Ibid., pp.283ff.

7. Martin Hengel, *Die Zeloten: Untersuchungen zur jüdischen Freiheitsbewegung in der Zeit von Herodes I bis 70 N. Chr.*, E.J. Brill, Leiden 1976.

8. Martin Hengel, *Was Jesus a Revolutionist?*, Fortress Press, Philadelphia 1971, p.33, translated from the German *War Jesus Revolutionar?*, Calwer Verlag, Stuttgart 1970.

9. O. Cullmann, *Jesus and the Revolutionaries*, Harper and Row, New York 1970.

10. Sigmund Mowinckel, *He That Cometh*, Blackwell and Abingdon, New York 1955, pp.4-6, 21ff.

11. Ibid., pp.96ff.

12. See for example, the Messianic Rule, in the Dead Sea Scrolls: Geza Vermes, *The Dead Sea Scrolls in English*, Penguin Books 1962, p.121.

13. Adalbert Merx, *Der Messias oder Ta'eb der Samaritaner,* A. Töpelmann, Giessen 1909.

14. IV Ezra 7, 26-44.

15. IV Ezra 13.

16. See Geza Vermes, *Jesus the Jew,* Collins 1973, pp.160-91.

17. See Albert Nolan, *Jesus Before Christianity: The Gospel of Liberation,* David Philip, Capetown 1976, pp.44-9.

18. Ibid., p.50.

19. There is an extensive literature on the trial of Jesus. See, for example, Paul Winter, *On the Trial of Jesus,* Walter de Gruyter, Berlin 1961; cf. E. Bammel (ed.), *The Trial of Jesus,* SBT II 13, SCM Press 1970.

II *Christology and Liberation Theology*

1. See the *Report of the Ecumenical Congress of Third World Theologians,* Sao Paulo, Brazil, 2 February – 2 March 1980, p.9.

2. Leonardo Boff, *Jesus Christ Liberator* (Portuguese 1972), Orbis Books, Maryknoll 1978 and SPCK 1979.

3. Jon Sobrino, *Christology at the Crossroads,* (Spanish 1976), Orbis Books, Maryknoll and SCM Press 1978.

4. José Miranda, *Being and the Messiah* (Spanish 1977), Orbis Books, Maryknoll 1979.

5. Luke 19.1-10.

6. See Albert Nolan, *Jesus Before Christianity: The Gospel of Liberation,* David Philip, Capetown 1976, pp.46f.

7. See Boff, *Jesus Christ Liberator,* pp.72f., 280-2.

8. The belief that a socialist alternative is necessary for liberation from poverty and oppression in Latin America and that this means that socialism is also closer to the kingdom of God 'as a system' may be said to be shared by most proponents of liberation theology, as well as other similar groups in Europe and North America, such as Christians for Socialism. See the volume on the first gathering for a joint North and Latin American liberation theology in Detroit, August 1975: *Theology in the Americas,* ed. Sergio Torres and John Eagleson, Orbis Books, Maryknoll 1976.

9. The concept of *La Raza* in Latin American and North American Hispanic liberation movements is significant. It locates the identity of the Latin American in the convergence of two or three cultures and peoples: European, Indian and African. From this there emerges the new 'race' as a people that brings together all peoples. This concept of *La Raza* allows the Latin American to claim both sides of his or her ethnic heritage, rather than just repudiating the European side for the side of the conquered African or Indian. See, for example, Matt Meier and Feliciano Rivera, *Readings on La Raza,* Hill and Wang, New York 1974.

10. I am indebted to Jon Sobrino for this link between the suffering of Jesus and the concrete 'reign of death' in Latin American society, particularly in El Salvador, in an informal talk given at the second conference of Theology in the Americas, Detroit, 4 August 1980.

11. There have been several challenges to Latin American liberation theology from European and Protestant theologians. One of the most famous of these was the open letter to José Miguez Bonino from Jürgen Moltmann, *Christianity and Crisis*, 26 March 1976.

12. This point was emphasized by Gustavo Gutierrez in the discussion leading up to the Third Latin American Bishops' Conference (CELAM III) and in his talk at the press conference at the Bishops' Conference in Puebla, Mexico, February 1979.

13. This point was made strongly in the talk by Sobrino in Theology of the Americas (see n.11 above). It would be a typical reply of liberation theology, in response to the prevalent Christian view of 'atheism'.

14. The theodicy question has been raised in relation to the Holocaust of the Jews in Richard Rubenstein, *After Auschwitz*, Bobbs Merrill, Indianapolis 1966. William R. Jones applied Rubenstein's work to the question of the unjustified sufferings of blacks in *Is God a White Racist?*, Anchor Books, Garden City, New York 1973.

15. I am again indebted to the talk of Jon Sobrino at Theology in the Americas (see n.11 above) for this analysis of why the El Salvadorean peasant does not raise the question of theodicy in relation to his or her unjust suffering.

16. The critique of the 'project of the poor', as Jon Sobrino called it, is much less developed in Latin American liberation theology than the critique of development and dependency. Sobrino stated in his talk (see n.11 above) that this will become necessary in due time (when successful revolutions become imminent).

17. Most liberation theologians would accept the legitimacy of a 'just war on the side of the revolution'. They would see this, not as a departure from Christian tradition but as the only valid application of the traditional concept of the 'just war'. There are some leading Latin American churchmen, such as Helder Camara, who take a pacifist position. While there is communication and understanding among Christians of the Left who take these two positions, there is no tolerance for Christians who, in the name of opposition to 'violence', support the unjust violence of the *status quo*.

III   *Christology and Jewish-Christian Relations*

1. Edward Flannery declares that the sources of Christian antisemitism are 'pagan hate'. This idea seems partly derived from the fact that Enlightenment figures, such as Voltaire, revived and used traditions of pagan antisemitism, regarding it as more respectable than Christian anti-Judaism. See Flannery, *The Anguish of the Jews*, Macmillan, New York 1964, pp.60f. For a discussion of this question see Rosemary Ruether, *Faith and Fratricide*, Seabury Press, New York 1974, pp.23-31.

2. Ibid., pp.183-225.

3. It is important to understand the two-sidedness of the Christian view

of the Jews, of both reprobation and preservation. Otherwise it is impossible to understand how the Jews survived in Christendom as the only allowable non-Christian or non-Orthodox religious option, despite the continual waves of persecution. In this respect religious anti-Judaism differs significantly from racial antisemitism which has no such motivation to 'preserve' the Jews. See Ruether, op.cit., p.185.

4. The question of the relationship between Christian anti-Judaism and racial antisemitism is a complex one. Some writers would deny any connection between the two. Others would see them as different languages for the same thing. A more appropriate view would seem to be one that recognizes important differences and yet significant cultural continuities. See Eva Fleischner, *Judaism in German Christian Theology since 1945*, Scarecrow Press, Metuchen, NJ, pp.23-7. Also the discussion in Alan Davies, *Antisemitism and the Foundations of Christianity*, Paulist Press, New York 1979, pp.188-207, 246-50.

5. This discussion follows substantially that of Chapter 5 of *Faith and Fratricide*, pp.226ff.

6. Ibid., pp.117-23. Cyprian's *Three Books of Testimonies against the Jews* would be a good example of a testimonies collection where the correlation of christological and anti-Judaic midrash of the scriptures can be clearly seen.

7. Küng characteristically identifies the Pharisees with 'legalism' and sees Jesus as being crucified 'by the Law'. See *On Being a Christian*, Doubleday, Garden City, NY and Collins 1966, pp.209-11, 241-4, 335. See also the dialogue between Küng and the Israeli scholar Pinchas Lapide in Hans Küng, *Signposts for the Future*, Doubleday, Garden City, NY and Collins 1978, p.74.

8. See Leonardo Boff, *Jesus Christ Liberator*, Orbis Books, Maryknoll 1978 and SPCK 1979, pp.67, 72-75, where the description of Pharisees as 'legalists' is equated with 'Judaism'.

9. See Asher Finkel, *The Pharisees and the Teacher of Nazareth*, E.J. Brill, Leiden 1964, pp.134-75.

10. For example, Hans Küng in his book *On Being a Christian* asks 'Why should one be a Christian?' He answers: 'In order to be truly human' (p.601). The obverse of this thesis would seem to be that non-Christians are less than fully human or less capable of becoming fully human.

11. GenR.34.8; see C.G. Montefiore and H. Loewe, *A Rabbinic Anthology*, Schocken Books, New York 1974, p.556.

12. Sifra 86b; see Montefiore, op.cit., p.564.

13. See, for example, The Community Rule, in the Dead Sea Scrolls: Geza Vermes, *The Dead Sea Scrolls in English*, Penguin Books 1962, pp.16ff.

14. See Montgomery Shroyer, *The Alexandrian Jewish Literalists*, Jewish Publication Society, Philadelphia 1936. See also the discussion in Ruether, *Faith and Fratricide*, p.37.

15. See for example Sidney Sowers, *The Hermeneutics of Philo and Hebrews*, TVZ Verlag, Zurich 1965, pp.89-127. This pattern of theological

comparison of the two covenants established in Hebrews becomes typical in the writings of the patristic period; see Ruether, *Faith and Fratricide,* pp.149ff.

16. Ellis Rivkin speaks of the Pharisees as creating a 'revolution' in Judaism which allowed it to survive the fall of the temple and the exile from the nation; see *The Shaping of Jewish History,* Scribner, New York 1971, pp.42ff.

17. Paul van Buren is an example of a Protestant theologian who has developed the concept of the proleptic nature of Jesus' messianic identity as a basis of Jewish-Christian relations, but would strictly reject any relativizing of Jesus as the sole source of salvation. See his *Discerning the Way: A Theology of the Jewish-Christian Reality,* Seabury Press, New York 1980.

IV   *Christology and Feminism*

1. Aquinas, *Summa Theologica,* Part I , Q 92, 1 and 2; Q 99,2; Part 3, Supplement, Q 39,1.

2. Augustine, *De Trinitate* 7,7,10.

3. Mary Daly, *Beyond God the Father,* Beacon Press, Boston 1973, p.19.

4. See, for example, John Saward, *Christ and his Bride,* Church Literature Association 1977.

5. *Declaration on the Question of the Admission of Women to the Ministerial Priesthood* 27, Vatican City, 15 October 1976.

6. A thorough critique of the Vatican *Declaration* by Catholic scholars can be found in *Women Priests: A Catholic Commentary on the Vatican Declaration,* edited by Arlene and Leonard Swidler, Paulist Press, New York 1977.

7. Naomi Goldenberg, *Changing of the Gods: Feminism and the End of Traditional Religion,* Beacon Press, Boston 1979, Chapter 1.

8. Zech.9.9f.; 14.1-21.

9. Aristotle, *Politics* I, 1-2.

10. See E. Goodenough, 'The Political Philosophy of Hellenistic Kingship', *Yale Classical Studies* I 1928.

11. See particularly Eusebius, *Oration on Constantine* passim.

12. See particularly Wisdom 6-9.

13. II Clement 12.2.

14. For Gnostic anthropology and male-female symbolism see Elizabeth Fiorenza, in R. Ruether (ed.), *Women of Spirit,* Simon and Schuster, 1979, 52-4; also Elaine Pagels, *The Gnostic Gospels,* Random House, New York 1979 and Weidenfeld and Nicolson 1980, pp.48-69.

15. See Jacob Boehme, *Mysterium Magnum: An Exposition of the First Book of Moses called Genesis,* translated by John Sparrow, John M. Watkins 1924, Vol.I, pp.121-33.

16. Julian of Norwich, *The Revelations of Divine Love,* Penguin Books 1973; see Eleanor McLaughlin, 'Christ, my Mother: Feminine Naming and Metaphor in Medieval Spirituality', *Nashotah Review* XV, 1975, pp.228-48.

17. See W. May, 'The Confession of Prous Boneta, Heretic and Heresiarch', in *Essays in Medieval Life and Thought Presented in Honor of Austin Patterson Evans*, New York 1955, pp.3-30.

18. Marjorie Reeves, *The Influence of Prophecy in the Later Middle Ages: A Study of Joachimism*, Clarendon Press 1969, pp.248-50 and notes.

19. *The Testimony of Christ's Second Appearing*, published by the United Society, called Shakers, Albany NY [4]1856, Book VIII, ch.9.1-38 and Book IX, ch.1,26–ch.2,30.

20. See Richard Pankhurst, *The Saint Simonians, Mill and Carlyle*, Humanities Press, Atlantic Highlands NJ 1957, ch.8.

21. Mary Baker Eddy, *Science and Health, With Key to the Scriptures*, Boston [86]1894, p.510.

22. The theme of the feminization of nineteenth-century American Christianity has been developed in a number of recent writings. See Ann Douglas, *The Feminization of American Culture*, Knopf, New York 1977. For the harnessing of the ideology of womanhood to feminist social reform see Rosemary Keller and Rosemary Ruether, *Women and Religion in America*, Vol. I, *The Nineteenth Century*, Harper and Row, San Francisco 1981, esp. chs. 6 and 7.

V Ecology and Human Liberation

1. The theme of 'lifeboat ethics' has particularly been popularized in the writings of Garrett Hardin. See the discussion in *Lifeboat Ethics: The Moral Dilemmas of World Hunger*, edited by George Lucas and Thomas Ogletree, Harper and Row, New York 1976.

2. See Martin Gellen, 'The Making of a Pollution-Industrial Complex', in *Eco-Catastrophe*, Ramparts editors, Harper and Row 1970, pp.73.ff.

3. The struggle over solar energy between decentralized, people-controlled technology and multi-national energy corporations has only begun. See John Keyes, *The Solar Conspiracy*, Morgan and Morgan, Dobbs Ferry 1978.

4. One of the dramatic stories of the interconnection of exploitation of labour and resources is told in Eduardo Galeano, *Open Veins of Latin America: Five Centuries of the Pillage of a Continent*, Monthly Review Press, New York 1973.

5. See Phyllis Trible, 'Images of Women in the Old Testament', in *Religion and Sexism*, edited by Rosemary Ruether, Simon and Schuster, New York 1974, pp.48-57.

6. Aristotle, *Politics* I, 1f.

7. Plato, *Republic* V, 452-7.

8. *Timaeus* 91.

9. Augustine, *Soliloquies* I, 10.

10. On ascetic egalitarianism of the sexes see Rosemary Ruether, *Women of Spirit*, Simon and Schuster, New York 1979, pp.71f.; also Elizabeth Clark, *Jerome, Chrysostom and Friends*, Edward Mellen Press,

New York and Toronto 1979, pp.35ff. The female appropriation of celibacy in early Christianity is also illustrated in Stevan Davies, *The Revolt of the Widows*, Southern Illinois University Press 1980.

11. See Lina Eckenstein, *Women under Monasticism, AD500—AD1500*, Cambridge University Press 1896.

12. See Friedrich Heer, *The Medieval World: Europe from 1100 to 1350*, Sphere Books 1974, pp.193ff. See also Lester Little, *Religious Poverty and the Profit Economy in Medieval Europe*, Cornell University Press, Ithaca, NY 1978.

13. Henri Pirenne, *Economic and Social History of Mediaeval Europe*, Harcourt, Brace and Co, New York 1937, pp.66-9.

14. The Faust legend has its roots in the mediaeval fear of the scientist as magician: see Grillot de Givry, *Witchcraft, Magic and Alchemy*, Dover Books, New York 1971, p.53.

15. 'Witches and Jews: Two Demonic Aliens', in Rosemary Ruether, *New Woman/New Earth: Sexist Ideologies and Human Liberation*, Seabury Press, New York 1975, pp.89-114.

16. Ernest Cassirer, *The Philosophy of the Enlightenment*, Beacon Press, Boston 1951, pp.37-92, 'Nature and Natural Science'.

17. R. Descartes, *Meditations on the First Philosophy, in which the Existence of God and the Distinction between Mind and Body are Demonstrated* (1641).

18. Comte and the Saint Simonians show how French positivism readily turns to seeing the scientist as a new 'clergy'.

19. Condorcet, *Sketch for a Historical Picture of the Progress of the Human Mind* (1793), especially 'The Tenth Stage'. See also Condorcet's plea for the citizenship of women, 'Speech before the French Revolutionary Assembly' (1789), in *The Fortnightly* 17 (1870), pp.719-29.

20. See Thomas F. Gossett, *Race: The History of an Idea in America*, Schocken Books, New York 1965, pp.144-75.

21. The rise of a new school of economics criticizing development theory and replacing it with a concept of 'dependence' has been fundamental to Latin American liberation theology. See Gustavo Gutierrez, *A Theology of Liberation*, Orbis Books, New York 1973 and SCM Press 1974, pp.81-7.

22. A classical statement of this is found in F. Engels, *Socialism: Utopian and Scientific* (1882), International Publishers, New York 1935, pp.68-73.

23. See Basil Willey, *The Eighteenth Century Background: The Idea of Nature*, Chatto and Windus and Columbia University Press, New York 1940, pp.205-11.

24. The matriarchal theory of origins was pioneered by writers such as J.J. Bachofen in the mid-nineteenth century, *Myth, Religion and Mother Right* (1861), Princeton University Press 1967.

25. See, for example, Theodore Roszak, *Where the Wasteland Ends*, Doubleday, New York 1973 and Faber and Faber 1974, pp.379.ff.

26. See my critique of Jung in Rosemary Ruether, *New Woman/New Earth*, pp.151-9.

27. The critique of hierarchical consciousness is creatively discussed in

Elizabeth Dodson Gray, *Why the Green Nigger? Remything Genesis*, Roundtable Press, Wellesley, Mass 1979.

28. Balance through diversity is often stated as a key principle of ecology: see Paul Ehrlich, *Human Ecology: Problems and Solutions*, W.H. Freeman, San Francisco 1973, p.6.

29. The interconnection of social justice and natural harmony is typically found in Near Eastern religious prayers. See, for example, Ivan Engnell, *Studies in Divine Kingship in the Ancient Near East*, Uppsala 1943, pp.43-5.

30. The connections between Canaanite patterns of renewal and Hebrew kingship ideology and messianic hope has been developed in numerous studies. See, for example, F.F. Hvidberg, *Weeping and Laughter in the Old Testament*, E.J. Brill, Leiden, 1962; also John Gray, *Near Eastern Mythology: Mesopotamia, Syria, Palestine*, Hamlyn, 1969, pp.115-35.

31. See Rosemary Ruether, 'The Biblical Vision of the Ecological Crisis', *Christian Century*, 22 November 1978, pp.1129-32.

32. The thesis that Jesus' messianic vision is, in reality, a Jubilee vision rather than an apocalyptic one has been suggested by John Howard Yoder, *The Politics of Jesus*, Eerdmans, Grand Rapids 1972, pp.64-78.

INDEX

INDEX